Effective Interaction With Patients

Ann Faulkner holds the first Chair of Communication Studies in Health Care at Sheffield University Medical School, and is Deputy Director of the Trent Palliative Care Centre, responsible for its day-to-day administration. She is involved in education and research in the areas of communication and counselling in Cancer and Terminal Care.

For Churchill Livingstone:

Publisher: Mary Law
Project Editor: Ellen Green
Editorial Co-ordination: Editorial Resources Unit
    Copy Editor: Anne-Marie Todkill
Production Controller: Nancy Henry
Design: Design Resources Unit
Sales Promotion Executive: Hilary Brown

Effective Interaction with Patients

Ann Faulkner PhD MLitt DipEd MA (Hons) SRN

Professor of Communication Studies in Health Care,
Deputy Director, Trent Palliative Care Centre, Sheffield

 CHURCHILL
LIVINGSTONE

EDINBURGH LONDON MADRID MELBOURNE NEW YORK AND TOKYO 1992

CHURCHILL LIVINGSTONE
Medical Division of Pearson Professional Ltd

Distributed in the United States of America by Churchill
Livingstone Inc., 650 Avenue of the Americas, New York,
N. Y. 10011, and by associated companies, branches and
representatives throughout the world.

First published 1992
    Reprinted 1995
    Reprinted 1996

ISBN 0-443-04226-8

British Library Cataloguing in Publication Data
A catalogue record for this book is available from the British
Library.

Library of Congress Cataloging in Publication Data
Faulkner, Ann.
    Improving nurse-patient interaction: a guide to effective
interaction with patients / Ann Faulkner.
        p.   cm.
    Includes bibliographical reference and index.
    ISBN 0–443–04226–8
    1. Nurse and patient.   2. Comminication in nursing.
3. Interpersonal communication.   I. Title.
    [DNLM: 1. Nurse-Patient Relations.   WY 87 F263i]
RT86.3F38   1992
610.73'06'99—dc20
DNLM/DLC
for Library of Congress   91–47921

The
publisher's
policy is to use
**paper manufactured
from sustainable forests**

Produced by Longman Singapore Publishers (Pte) Ltd
Printed in Singapore

Preface

When I first became concerned, in the early 1970s, about communication in health care, I found little sympathy from teaching colleagues. I well remember a senior colleague saying, 'Oh Ann, you are going to be one of those who advocate understanding the patient while he quietly bleeds to death.'

Fortunately, attitudes have changed and communication as a subject has become more important in both nursing and medical curricula. Much work has yet to be done but the professions themselves are asking how they can interact more effectively with patients, relatives and colleagues, and in at least one medical school (Sheffield) an annual prize is awarded to the medical student showing most ability in interviewing skills.

This is a practical book, putting communication into context for health professionals. It is based on the work I developed in working with nurses and on the (later) work which was jointly developed by Peter Maguire and myself in multidisciplinary workshops on cancer and terminal care.

The book is illustrated with vignettes from real case studies, to show the effects of different strategies on interactions and to illustrate the use of key skills.

I have enjoyed writing this little book and make no apologies for its pragmatic approach.

Sheffield 1992   Ann Faulkner

Acknowledgements

Without the support and enthusiasm of family, colleagues and friends, this book would not have been written. Peter Maguire in particular has influenced the way my thinking has developed from the early days, when we began to refine our ideas and work on a joint model of assessment in cancer care.

A.F.

Contents

For the Man within the Child
Thank you

1

The need for effective interaction

ASSESSMENT

Assessment is the first stage of the medical interview and of the nursing process, which is often described as a problem-solving approach to patient care. The assessment stage allows us to **identify** problems, and it could be argued that since it is over-optimistic to expect to solve all problems, we only need to know about those requiring a medical or nursing intervention. Such a view is held by many nurses who feel a failure when faced with seemingly intractable problems that they themselves cannot deal with. For them, there is safety in having a standard nursing assessment form where well-defined potential problems are listed, and require only a tick in an appropriate box.

Patient presents with problem
↓
Assessment by health professional
↓
Identify problems
↓
Agree goals with patient

Fig. 1.1 Assessment as the first stage of patient care planning

This book is about effective interaction with individual people who have individual problems. Some of these problems may be familiar to those who care for the patient, while others will be unfamiliar in themselves or in their manifestations. Once elicited, some problems may have no immediate solution. The argument will be made here, however, that if the best possible care is to be given, all problems that a patient is prepared to disclose are of importance in building a picture of where he 'is at' with respect to coping with his disease and its treatment.

Joanna Hope provides a test case for this total approach. Joanna is 35, married, and has two young sons of 5 and 7 years. She is in hospital for a hysterectomy due to heavy bleeding during her periods. At an interview, Joanna discloses a number of problems, which include a violent husband. This knowledge (which would probably have remained hidden without effective interaction) is of considerable importance in planning Joanna's care. It will help to ensure that important concerns — i.e. her sons' welfare when she is not there to protect them and her own well-being during her convalescent period at home — are addressed. The argument that it is not necessary to know of her husband's violence since it is not directly relevant to her surgery does not stand. Joanna may need counselling and intervention if appropriate, and perhaps a period of convalescence before going home.

The hardest part of finding out what problems patients have is in having to watch them make 'informed' decisions which may not be the most appropriate. At a physical level this may mean refusing a blood transfusion on religious grounds and at an emotional level remaining with a marriage partner who is obviously having a deleterious effect on both physical and mental health. Learning that logical solutions are not necessarily accepted by patients should, however, help to foster the notion that individuals should generate their own solutions where possible.

Communication needs to be effective so that care can be planned on the basis of the patient's authentic problems, rather than on what we *think* are his problems. Research suggests that most nurses do not exhibit the skills required for effective assessment (Faulkner 1980, Macleod Clark 1982). The same holds true for doctors (Maguire et al 1978). What is encouraging, however, is that in experimental studies both nurses

and doctors improve their skills dramatically after brief training (Maguire 1982, Faulkner & Maguire 1984).

Barriers to effective assessment

Lack of skills

From the above, it can be seen that one barrier to effective interaction is a lack of skills on the part of health professionals. For example, 'closed' and 'leading' questions will direct the focus of a patient's reply and restrict him to preferred responses, as in the following exchange:

Nurse: Hello, Mr Smith, I've come to see if you have any worries about your operation.

Mr Smith: Well . . .

Nurse: The doctor has explained it all to you, hasn't he?

Mr Smith: Well . . .

Nurse: Good! So you won't have a lot of worries, will you?

Mr Smith: (doubtfully) No.

Nurse: I'll tell you what will happen so you won't be frightened.

The nurse goes on to explain the procedure before and after the operation. She does not discover that Mr Smith is very frightened because a close friend died while on the operating table. It will be seen in Chapter 4 that there are key skills which allow such worries to be elicited. These include, in addition to questioning techniques, other important skills which can ensure that each individual has the opportunity to disclose his real concerns.

Making assumptions

Another common barrier to effective interaction is that health professionals tend to make assumptions about the individual. This is easily understood, since experience can suggest typical problems associated with any particular condition. It is an easy step from previous experience to an assumption that certain patients will have certain problems. For example, women with cervical cancer may have sexual problems and fears of recurrence (Walker 1990). It is a temptation to assume that any patient with cervical cancer who seems worried has these problems. This can result in other concerns being missed unless open questions are asked.

The same set of assumptions can operate, in that because there are common problems associated with a particular diagnosis, those problems may be imposed on all patients with that diagnosis. If this is dealt with in an unskilled way, self-fulfilling prophecy may result in that a patient may feel that if other patients are worried, then perhaps he should be worried too. It is not unusual to hear a patient say, 'I hadn't thought of worrying about my looks, but perhaps it will show, and other people will notice. Oh dear. . .'

A golden rule in talking to patients is to make *no* assumptions prior to, or during, an interview. This is difficult because in daily experience what psychologists call 'set' operates in order that we run our lives smoothly. The notion of 'set' derives from the fact that certain experiences are repeated time and time again as individuals go about their daily business. Examples of this are getting out of bed in the morning, making tea or coffee, and walking in and out of buildings. After a point such actions can be repeated without conscious thought. The next step is to generalize the behaviour to other, similar situations.

A good example of this is in opening doors. Most doors have a handle that turns, and open by pushing *into* a room. If, however, the door opens *outwards*, 'set' can get in the way and result in an individual pushing hard at a door and feeling a bit silly when someone comes along, says 'excuse me', and proceeds to open the door by turning the handle and pulling outwards. Each patient should be interviewed as if he is the door that opens outwards; the interviewer's past experience may help to identify problems, but it should not be allowed to exclude the individuality of each human being.

Distancing

Some of the research already cited shows that many health professionals distance themselves from patients and their families. Interactions are brief and superficial, and any potentially 'difficult' material is blocked. The interviewer may cause this 'blocking' by ignoring what the individual is saying or by giving premature reassurance. Imagine that Mr Smith is able to verbalize his fears of dying on the operating table:

Mr Smith: My friend died in the theatre, you know.

Nurse: Well, you don't need to worry about that! I've never lost a patient yet.

Mr Smith: But it obviously *can* happen.

Nurse: Now, now! No need to be morbid. You are in very good hands.

Here Mr Smith is being prevented from exploring his concerns with the nurse and may be left feeling silly or guilty (or both) about his fears.

Why should there be a need to distance in this and other ways? One explanation seems to be the fear of 'getting in too deep'. This may be related to the idea that health professionals solve problems. To return to the example of Mr Smith, it is not possible to promise that there is absolutely *no* chance of him dying in theatre. The nurse can, however, allow him to talk through his fears and perhaps help to minimize them, by asking the anaesthetist to talk to him and by giving realistic reassurance. Until an in-depth interview is undertaken it will be impossible to discover how many parallels there are between Mr Smith and his friend, or the real depth of the worry.

Another very real reason for distancing is the cost to the carer in terms of how much of another's concerns and pain can be tolerated in any one day. If assessment is superficial, there is less chance of being drawn into the other person's world. Distancing can give the interviewer a sense of safety. This question of the health professional's 'survival' will be considered in Chapter 10, as there is a need for health workers to understand their own limits so that they can offer the best care possible to all patients and their families.

Personal distancing. Sometimes a particular individual will 'trigger' a painful or unpleasant memory in the health professional. Sometimes these 'triggers' operate at an unconscious level but it is always worth looking for possible reasons when distancing occurs that is specific to a particular patient or patient group. Currently, patients who are HIV positive induce distancing tactics in many health professionals due to connotations of sexual deviance and drug abuse, but when those professionals are asked to examine their feelings they often discover other dimensions to their aversion which are more personal. Self-awareness can reduce such specific distancing or alert the carer to the need for 'time out' in some way. For example, if a health professional is recently bereaved, he or she may find it difficult to return immediately to the area of terminal care. Accepting this, rather than subscribing to the common belief that those in health care can always 'cope', can help the carer to survive to return when he or she has adapted to the loss.

'Time out' to avoid this type of distancing can mean a change of speciality for a while, a short break, or counselling, depending on the reason for the 'trigger'. Sometimes, if the distancing is specific to one person, then what may be needed is the honesty to accept that the doctor or nurse is not the best person to care for that patient. It is a fallacy to believe that all patients will engender equal concern, and more realistic to accept that, inevitably, difficulty will be experienced from time to time in relating to particular patients or relatives.

Selective listening. A more subtle form of distancing is by the use of selective listening. Again, this may not occur at a conscious level but it will almost certainly prevent the patient from sharing his concerns, for when his cues (see Ch. 4) are repeatedly ignored, he is educated to realize that certain topics are taboo.

It may be, for example, that the nurse who interviewed Joanna Hope did not know how to respond to her personal disclosures. The interaction may then have been affected, and real problems left undisclosed. Consider the following exchange:

> Joanna: I'm worried about having to be in hospital.

> Nurse: Worried?
> Joanna: About my boys.
> Nurse: I'm sure they will be fine.
> Joanna: Well — my husband isn't always patient with them — in fact . . .
> Nurse: (cutting in) Now, now, you have got to concentrate on getting better. I'm sure your husband will manage — do him good.
> Joanna: I worry, and I'm not sure how he will be when I'm home.
> Nurse: You mothers! Now, let's talk about you — you will have to be very careful when you go home — get hubby to help.
> Joanna: But that's the problem . . .
> Nurse: You have spoilt them all — I can tell — I'll talk to him when he visits.
> Joanna: (resigned) Well — alright.

In this interaction, Joanna's cues are all missed by the nurse, perhaps because of the nurse's desire to reassure in addition to her inability to deal with personal disclosures.

Doing harm

Another barrier to effective interaction, linked to the above, is a fear on the part of health professionals that if they encourage disclosure of problems, they may do more harm than good. For example, the patient who is dealing with a fear-provoking diagnosis and resultant uncertainty may have many insoluble problems. A common argument from health professionals is that to allow the patient to explore those concerns would be counter-productive in that he could become depressed and lose hope as he becomes fully aware of the situation. Much better, it is argued, to maintain hope and optimism by underplaying the seriousness of the situation.

In this, relatives often encourage and collude with health professionals. They maintain that the patient should be protected from reality, even to the extent that direct questions should not be answered. This may cause more problems for the patient, who is trying to make sense of what is happening. It may also cause problems for staff and relatives since it can be a strain to keep a secret. In terminal care, there may be further problems if a patient dies leaving unfinished business and the relatives have had no chance to say goodbye or to make decisions with their loved one's approval.

The notion that effective interaction, which allows an individual to identify and explore his problems, can do harm, is related to the professional's belief that he or she is the strong protector of the weak. In fact, most patients are not weak. It will be seen in Chapter 6 that the skilled interviewer is able to negotiate the depth and content of an interview so that patients are not harmed.

Provoking strong emotions

There is a fear among health professionals that to encourage the disclosure of problems may provoke strong emotions which they will be unable to handle. These may include anger, guilt and hostility. The problem here is within the health professional and can be overcome by learning strategies for helping the patient deal with his emotions. Such strategies are discussed in some detail in Chapter 7.

The patient can benefit by 'getting things off his chest', for anger needs to be defused and guilt and hostility need to be explored in a non-judgemental way. The anxiety surrounding such disclosures is generally followed by a feeling of relief, as in the following exchange:

Nurse: I thought you were rather upset when we talked the other day. It must be hard to accept that things don't look too good.

Mrs Walsh: Well, I had wanted to bring it into the open — but yes — I found talking about it very worrying. I had a good cry after you left.

Nurse: And now?

Mrs Walsh: I'm coming to grips with it — sorting things out — and in a funny way, more at peace with

myself. There is nothing worse than being unsure. Now I know what I'm dealing with — even if I don't like it much.

Documentation

It may appear strange to cite documentation as a barrier to effective interaction, but patient records as used by both nursing and medical personnel can reduce the interview to no more than a check-list of closed questions. Both medical and nursing process histories tend to follow a physical pattern which, if followed without skill, allows little time or opportunity for a patient to disclose any but the most fundamental concerns. For example, a nurse using a 'process' assessment form may not get beyond a superficial level of questioning in her interview:

Nurse: Mrs Hope, is it OK if I ask you a few questions? It will help us plan your care.

Joanna: That's fine by me.

Nurse: Good. Can you tell me what you expect to happen here?

Joanna: I know I have to have an operation for my fibroids.

Nurse: Fine — and that has been explained?

Joanna: Yes.

Nurse: Good. Now I need to ask some questions about your health. Do you have any breathing problems?

Joanna: No.

Nurse: And you don't smoke?

Joanna: No.

Nurse: What about diet?

Joanna: Well — it's normal.

Nurse: And do you drink?

Joanna: Yes.

Nurse: (laughing) But you don't tipple?

Joanna: No.

It is clear that Joanna would be given little opportunity in an assessment of this sort to divulge either social or psychological concerns.

Many of the barriers to effective assessment that have been described here can be overcome if health professionals are taught the skills and strategies for effective interaction. These are dealt with in depth in other chapters of the book.

Patient interviews – general considerations

Nature of the interview

The aim of interviewing a patient is firstly to identify his problems and from the information gathered formulate plans for care. The traditional approach to this was for the doctor to take a medical history and then to tell other members of the health care team the care that was necessary for a particular patient. The advent of the nursing process (Roper et al 1980) was seen by many doctors as an attempt on the part of nurses to erode their role as decision-makers. In fact, what nurses were arguing was that a nursing history is different from a medical history, and rather than erode the doctor's role, they were hoping to complement it.

On a busy surgical ward in the Midlands, in the early days of the nursing process, a Sister attached nursing histories to the patients' case notes. The consultant came to do a round and rather than read the histories, as Sister had hoped, detached them and dropped them into the bin. On the day of the next round the Sister tried again. This time a lighted match followed the histories.

A salutary tale, though happily such prejudice has largely disappeared as doctors and nurses work towards a team approach. What remains is the difficulty of establishing who should interview the patient, when, and on what topics. It would be easy to argue that doctors take a history of the disease while nurses are more concerned with reactions to the disease. This is over-simplistic, since both professions should be concerned with the whole person, that is, with his or her physical, social and psychological concerns.

The difference between medical and nursing interviews lies in their respective emphases; the

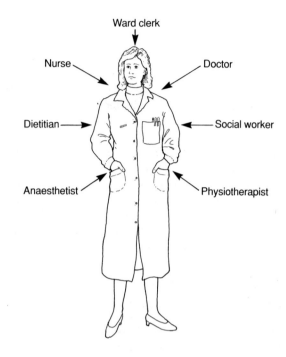

Fig. 1.2   Who should interview the patient?

doctor's prime aim is to make a diagnosis and prescribe effective treatment to cure, control or palliate, while the nurse needs to identify problems, which may affect care. Of course, doctors may identify 'nursing' problems while nurses may identify problems that are more 'medical' in nature. This means that the best patient care is that to which both doctor and nurse have contributed as part of a team.

A team approach

In reality, the patient often feels that too many professionals have asked the same questions. George, an elderly pensioner, had been admitted with an enlarged prostate gland. He is obviously undernourished and is also bronchitic. On the day of admission, a nurse interviews him using a nursing process approach. He admits to being short of money, eating sparsely, breathing with difficulty and to a variety of associated problems. Not least of these is that his wife has died recently and he is unable to face the reality of this without extreme pain. As a result, he keeps a tight rein on his emotions and has not expressed his grief.

The following morning, the doctor interviews him and again he gives his history, albeit with a more physical emphasis. Later the dietician visits to assess and plan for dietary needs, and following that, the physiotherapist. That evening, the nurse takes George his supper and asks if he is expecting any visitors that evening. He erupts and sends the nurse scurrying as he says: 'Don't you start . . . . Questions, questions . . . all bloody questions — how much more do you all want to know?'

George has a point, but so does each professional involved in his care. One way to protect patients from too many people asking the same questions is for the team to share information. This allows each professional to avoid overlap. If, for example, the nurse, after her assessment, shares her information with the doctor, he may then approach George in a different way — for although he would need to make his own assessment, he could acknowledge that a nursing history has been taken and explain why he needs to explore further particular areas. This does not mean that on a first visit, the patients' concerns are not explored. Rather, that it may not be possible with all patients to explore those concerns fully. If stress appears to block disclosure, the health professional may need to negotiate a second visit for a more detailed assessment.

Timing

Admission to hospital is known to be a time of high stress for patients (Wilson-Barnett 1979), and this is probably also true of the first house visit or appointment at the health centre. The aim of the first interaction should be to engender trust so that the patient feels able to disclose as much as he is able. And patients will vary enormously in their ability to give a coherent story.

In hospital, the first assessment should be delayed until the patient has settled into the ward. The nurse may take the patient to his bed and explain the layout and general routine of the ward. Then the patient can be left to get the feel of the ward, perhaps by chatting with another patient; he can then be interviewed after lunch. By then, hopefully, he will feel ready to start giving the nurse his reactions to his current situation.

The above sets out an ideal. In real life other forces may militate against this. For example, the terminally ill patient may have little time left when he is admitted to hospital or hospice but may still need to talk. It will be seen in Chapter 4 that there are ways to monitor the patient's ability to disclose his concerns and feelings.

Under no circumstances should multiple interviews be conducted in one day. Nor should it be expected that the patient's complete story will be divulged in one interview. Assessment is a dynamic and ongoing process and, given that there are almost always time constraints, the patient should be encouraged to prioritize problems.

Expectation of problems

The reason for admission to hospital or a home visit is usually established before either of these take place; thus, the patient's physical problem will have been identified before nursing intervention begins. The problem solving approach, however, has been described as a problem identification approach to care; this leads to the expectation that all patients have problems.

Sarah, a junior nurse, had been trusted to do her first interview with a patient. She later returned to Sister in near tears, explaining that she had failed to find any problems except the one that the patient had been admitted for. The patient, Lilian Woodruffe, was admitted for planned removal of a non-malignant mole on her face. She had a supportive family and had been able to make adequate arrangements for her time in hospital. She is stable and happy with no more than the day-to-day concerns of any normal individual.

Sarah, the nurse, had made a clear and concise assessment of the patient, and was reassured by Sister that only a proportion of patients have social and emotional problems which need attention.

Summary

In this introduction, the importance of effective interaction with patients has been explored, along with some of the barriers to communication that may be created by health professionals, such as a low level of skill, making assumptions, distancing and fear of the consequences of encouraging an individual to articulate his concerns. Problems have also been highlighted in the areas of the risk of duplicating patient interviews, and the timing of interviews, given that newly diagnosed patients are often under considerable stress.

REFERENCES

Faulkner A 1980 The student nurses' role in giving information to patients. Unpublished M Litt thesis, University of Aberdeen
Faulkner A, Maguire P 1984 Teaching assessment skills. In: Faulkner A (ed) Recent advances in nursing — 7. Communication. Churchill Livingstone, Edinburgh.
Macleod Clark J 1982 Nurse–patient verbal interaction. Unpublished Ph D thesis, University of London.
Maguire P, Roe P, Goldberg D, Jones, S Hyde C, O'Dowd T 1978 The value of feedback in teaching interviewing skills to medical students. Psychological Medicine 8: 698–704
Maguire P 1982 Doctor–patient skills in social skills and health. Methuen, London p 55–81
Roper N, Logan W, Tierney A 1980 The elements of nursing. Churchill Livingstone, Edinburgh
Walker A 1990 The problems of patients with cervical cancer. In: Faulkner A (ed) Oncology. Sevtain Press, London
Wilson-Barnett J 1979 Stress in hospital. Churchill Livingstone, Edinburgh p 25–33

EXERCISES

1. Think of a patient whom you have interviewed in the last month and then jot down the following:

   a. Physical problems which you identified

   b. Psychological problems which you identified

   c. Social problems which you identified.

   With hindsight, what information would you need that was not disclosed at the time?

2. List any barriers which affect the way that you interview patients; then plan ways in which they can be overcome.

2

Preparing for an assessment interview

NEGOTIATING THE INTERVIEW

Given that the assessment interview will set the scene for planning care, thought should be given to where and when the interview will take place, the time that will be required, and any factors which will help the patient to cooperate and disclose current problems.

The ideal

In an ideal world an assessment interview would not take place unless privacy was assured, there was absolutely no chance of interruption, and time was as flexible as required.

Privacy

Whether the patient is assessed in his own home, in a clinic or in hospital, privacy is a natural requirement. Privacy with no distractions can help a patient feel safer than if he were in an open ward with other people present who might appear to be listening. A safe environment can help disclosure of problems and concerns in a way that is not possible otherwise. Ideally, the room where the interview takes place should be tranquil and quiet so that the patient and the interviewer may sit comfortably without fear of disturbance.

Interruptions should be kept to a minimum. If there is a telephone in the room then the interviewer should make arrangements for calls to be diverted during the period of assessment. A notice similar to those in hotel rooms can be put on the door to show that the people in the room do not wish to be disturbed. Finally, the interviewer should explain to her colleagues that an interview is about to take place and that she and the patient will not be available for the projected period of time. All these steps will avoid interruptions which could have an effect on the patient's willingness to disclose.

Timing

In preparing for an assessment interview, the health professional should allow enough time for the interview to be as complete as possible. There are wide variations in belief as to how long an assessment interview should be. For example, many nurses are taught to give the impression that they have 'all the time in the world', when in fact no one has all the time in the world. Workloads are such that time has to be apportioned among competing demands. What is important is that the time available is made clear to the patient so that he does not have unrealistic expectations. This will be discussed further in Chapter 3.

If it is possible to allow 20 minutes to half an hour for an interview, most patients will feel that this is a reasonable amount of time. The average general practitioner interview, for example, is less than 8 minutes, and it is a fact that even in a relatively short time, the patient, with a skilled interviewer, can give a clear and reasonable history of his problems and current concerns. It is also true that the patient who feels that his story is going to take much longer than the time being offered should be able to say 'Twenty minutes isn't any good to me', so that the necessary time can be negotiated.

The reality

The reality that the professional faces when planning an assessment interview is usually far from the ideal. Many wards do not have a private room where a patient can be interviewed. People in their own homes often cannot locate an area where they can be alone with the health worker who visits them, and health centres often lack privacy except in the general practitioners' offices.

Telephones ring, 'Do Not Disturb' notices are ignored, children rush in and out and occasionally a partner tries to insist on remaining present when the patient is assessed.

Privacy

In hospital. Although hospital wards are often divided into small bays rather than arranged as Nightingale wards, there still may be problems of privacy. In a four-bedded bay, for example, the distance between one bed and the next may be no more than the width of a locker and the rail for the curtains.

In such a situation, the best that can be achieved may be an illusion of privacy. Most patients speak very quietly and if the nurse or doctor is sitting close to the bed or chair, a conversation can occur in which the patient will disclose worries and concerns, feeling relatively safe. Indeed, many would argue that the patient is more comfortable in his own bed with his own things on his locker, rather than being taken off to a neutral room, where he may feel uncomfortable and perhaps apprehensive about what is going to happen.

It is important to let colleagues know that an assessment interview is taking place, in order to minimize interruptions during the assessment. Similarly, it is desirable to avoid being called to the telephone or to deal with another situation that will break the flow of the interview.

If the ward does have a private room where the patient can be taken, it may be most effective if the patient is given the option of whether the interview takes place at the bedside or in the family or interviewing room that is available. This is one of the many situations where the patient's perspective is all-important.

At home. There is an old belief that when visiting a patient in his own home the nurse or doctor is indeed a visitor who is there at the patient's wish and therefore must adopt the rules of the patient's house. Such a belief can result in an interview taking place in a room with the television on, animals running around, children

Table 2.1 Checklist for privacy with patients

Setting	Action
In hospital clinic:	Divert telephone calls Inform colleagues Use 'Do Not Disturb' sign Clear enough time
In patient's home:	Make appointment Make clear contract to see patient alone Inform colleagues Leave 'bleep' in car

demanding attention, and many other interruptions and distractions.

In fact, the health professional is *not* a visitor in the social sense. He or she is there offering a professional service in professional terms. This gives the health professional the right to ask, for example, that the television be switched off, or to negotiate for somewhere quiet and separate for the interview to take place. The best preparation of all in this circumstance is to telephone ahead and negotiate the time and duration of the visit and to arrange for it to take place in some degree of privacy.

Patients can normally make arrangements so that they can be seen alone, particularly if the health professional makes it clear that this is important. It may be, for example, that there are times when the children are at school or playgroup and their father at work, so that Mum can be seen on her own. What is often difficult to arrange is that a partner does not attend, even though he or she particularly wants to. Again, the professional needs to negotiate this quite firmly; while accepting the concern of the relative, he or she must make it explicit that the interview is primarily for the patient, but that there will be an opportunity for patient and partner to be seen together at a later date.

An unexpected home visit can cause problems for the patient and his family. It may be, for example, that there is a spare room but that it is not heated because it is used only for special occasions.

The presence of a partner. One problem that is very difficult to deal with is that of a partner who is not only disinclined to leave his or her loved one alone with the nurse or doctor but is actually insistent about staying. This happens particularly in clinics where the partner has accompanied the patient, and in the home when the partner is the main carer for the patient. Consider the following exchange:

Nurse: Hello, Mr Waters I am the Macmillan nurse; I have come to see your wife.

Mr Waters: Come in Nurse, I'll take you up.

Nurse: If you just show me where her room is, Mr Waters.

Mr Waters: Oh no, I'm coming in with you.

Nurse: Well I am quite happy to talk to you later, either alone or with your wife, but on this first visit it is important that I talk to her alone and get an idea of her concerns and worries.

Mr Waters: She won't say anything that I can't hear.

Nurse: That may be true but I do please ask you to let me talk to your wife alone first, and then I will talk to you.

Mr Waters: Well, I suppose so. Maisie, here's the nurse come to see you, says she wants to see you on her own, I'll be downstairs waiting.

In this exchange Mr Waters is very reluctant to leave his wife alone with the nurse; nevertheless, he does concede and the nurse makes sure after the interview that she talks to him about his concerns and offers to see him together with his wife at a later time.

If a partner absolutely insists on being there then the professional may have no choice but to conduct the interview in the presence of the partner. This may well inhibit the amount of disclosure as patient and partner seek to protect each other. To maximize the chance of a proper assessment being made, the terms of a visit should always be negotiated. But the health professional should not expect 100% success, as there are always people who resist even the most expert negotiation.

Handling interruptions. Perhaps more disconcerting than the persistent partner is the interrupter. The carer may accept that the interview is with the patient alone, but keep appearing at the door offering cups of tea or other diversions. Again it is important to negotiate and to make it clear to the carer that the interview should not be interrupted. This is best done sooner rather than later, even though it may seem a little bit authoritarian.

Mr Waters:	Go on in then Nurse, I will bring you up a cup of tea in a few minutes.
Nurse:	I'd love a cup of tea after the interview if I've got time, but I'd rather we weren't interrupted while I'm talking to your wife.
Mr Waters:	But she always has a cup of tea about now and I don't want her to wait.
Nurse:	Well, why don't you give me the tea and I will take it in to her when I go.
Mr Waters:	I suppose so.

In this exchange Mr Waters is not pleased to have his reason for interrupting taken away, but by being clear about the ground rules for the visit, the nurse is able to earn his respect. Over the period of time that she visits Mrs Waters she will develop a very good relationship with both the patient and her husband.

A more difficult interruption is that of children or animals rushing in or out of the room. This needs to be dealt with tactfully but firmly if the interview is to proceed smoothly.

Timing

In reality it may be quite difficult for a nurse or doctor to ensure enough time for an assessment interview. It may be that a nurse wants to assess a patient and feels that it would take half an hour. She may do all the right things. She may negotiate with colleagues, negotiate with the patient, check that the phone is not going to interrupt, and ensure that she will not be called away to other jobs. In spite of all this, things can go wrong, and an interview be disrupted. In such a situation, if it is absolutely crucial that the interview be brought to an end, then renegotiation will have to take place for the interview to be concluded at another time.

Similarly, in the home or clinic, the child who should have been at playgroup may have an upset tummy or a temperature; a friend may have come to visit unexpectedly, not knowing that the health professional was to call; and few people are strong-minded about pulling the plug out on the telephone to ensure privacy. In situations like this, even though time will be lost, it is preferable to renegotiate another visit rather than attempt to assess someone when she is worried about a sick child, or where a third person is present and seems disinclined to leave. By renegotiating in this way the patient can be helped to realize how important the requested time alone is.

Many interruptions occur in assessment interviews because not all staff give due priority to this area of care. Patients are assessed using tick-lists and nurses and doctors are still nervous of encouraging a patient to disclose feelings. In making appropriate time for an assessment interview, health professionals need to be much more assertive about their need for time and privacy with a particular patient.

OTHER PREPARATION
Reviewing available information

When the time and place of an interview have been negotiated, other preparation is required; this includes finding out what information is available about the patient. Notes and letters of referral will give some sort of picture of a patient's background, history, and current condition. There are, however, pros and cons to having information prior to an interview with a new patient.

Pros

It can make a patient feel very comfortable to discover that the person who is interviewing him actually knows something about him. Such foreknowledge shows interest in the patient and his problems in that the health professional has taken the trouble to gain some background information.

Doctor:	Hello, Mr West?
Mr West:	Yes, that's me.
Doctor:	I understand you have come into hospital because you have got a few problems, not feeling too well I understand; I see you work at Mill Hill Supplies?
Mr West	(looking pleased) Yes, that's right. I've been shop floor manager there for, oh, the last 10 years.
Doctor:	And these problems are affecting your sleep and your waterworks.
Mr West:	That's right.

In this exchange Mr West feels that the doctor knows something about him and about the sort of problems he has been having. He is simply able to confirm the picture that the doctor has built up.

At visiting time Mr West is full of praise for the doctor, and tells his wife: 'You know, it's amazing, I've never been in this hospital before and yet they seem to know all about me, even where I work. You trust people like that when they take an interest.' It can be seen that having knowledge of the patient and his concerns at the time of admission can boost the patient's confidence in the staff and in their ability to help him.

Cons

The difficulty of knowing about the patient's concerns on admission, or on the first visit, is that it can close the mind to other equally important problems. In Mr West's case the doctor knows what he does for a living, what his health record is and what his current physical problem is. This could be seen to get in the way of identifying other less obvious problems. This is similar to selective listening (see p. 4). In terminal care, for example, people are often admitted to a hospice for pain control. A letter of referral may well give prominence to the pain as a reason for

admission. Without an in-depth assessment, the patient's pain may be treated while underlying and associated problems remain unidentified:

Doctor:	Well, Mr Rutland, I understand you are in here for us to sort your pain.
Mr Rutland:	Well, I have had a few problems.
Doctor:	We will soon get you sorted, it is one of the things we are very good at here.

Here the doctor is concentrating on the stated reason for admission. Mr Rutland, however, has a number of worries on his mind. This is his first admission to a hospice and he has a lot of preconceptions about hospice care and what it entails. He has been coming to grips with the reality that he will not live for very much longer, and much of his pain is mental. This will require very careful assessment in order that unanswered questions can be dealt with and other concerns addressed.

The difficulty, then, of having too much preknowledge of a patient is that it can militate against the patient's being encouraged to tell his own story. If a clear letter of referral with all relevant details is used as a basis for treatment, without anything more than reiteration from the patient that these are his problems, the assessment interview, when it occurs, may be very physically orientated rather than physical, psychological and social in content.

Using available information constructively

Available information can be very useful as long as it is used constructively. An effective way to use available information about a patient is to hold it in the background while still, at assessment, asking the patient to tell his story in his own words according to his own perceptions. This will give a clear picture of the patient's understanding of what is happening to him and show up any mismatch between what the patient believes and what the referring doctor believes about his problems and concerns. Mr Rutland, for example, when encouraged to tell his own story, shows that although he is in pain and his doctor feels that this would be better dealt with in the hospice setting, he has other concerns which for him have much higher priority. What Mr Rutland had not realized was that the pain he was feeling was related to the other concerns in his life.

Coordinating competing interviews

Having prepared for an assessment interview, set a time and a place and become au fait with available information, it is worthwhile to check whether other interviews have either taken place in the very near past or are scheduled to take place in the immediate future. If, for example, a long medical interview has recently taken place or is due to take place, then the nursing interview could be postponed to another day, so that the patient does not feel overwhelmed with questions and attention. Notes of recent interviews, if they are available, can give added factual information that may help health professionals to make sure that they do not cover too much similar ground while yet gaining the information that they need for their own understanding of the patient's problems, and to complete their records.

At a very simple level, if the records show clearly the patient's name, date of birth and address it would be very irritating to the patient to have those questions asked again. What is required, however, is for the information to be confirmed as correct.

Finally, because a number of health professionals require specific information from a patient, it is important to explain the exact nature of each interview. This helps the patient to understand that everybody is not repeating the same task. For example, a dietitian may need to talk to Mr West in considerable depth about his dietary habits, whereas in an overall nursing assessment the major concern would be not so much the itemized detail that the dietitian requires but some sense of what a normal diet is for Mr West. In this respect the patient is the barometer of the effectiveness of the interview, and may show irritation in response to repeated questions.

Mr West told his wife that everybody seemed to know his or her job. He then simplified matters enormously by telling his wife that 'The doctor was wanting to make sure that he gave me the right treatment; the dietitian, well she wanted to make sure that I get my food right.' Mrs West then asked, 'Well, but what about the nurse — what did she want?' Mr West replied, 'Oh she just wants to look after me, she needs to know what I want and how I feel.' This simple segregation is, of course, far from the full reality of a team approach, but to Mr West each person had an allotted job, and he was quite happy with that. Each professional had gained the information that he or she required in a way that was acceptable to the patient.

Summary

In this chapter, preparation required for an assessment interview has been considered in terms of the ideal as far as privacy and timing are concerned, and the reality, which may be very different. Some of the problems that may occur, and ways of dealing with these, have been considered. Although it has been accepted that there are occasionally problems that cannot be overcome, the value of negotiation and pre-arrangement has been stressed. The pros and cons of using available information have been considered, along with the organization of interviews such that no patient has multiple interviews in one day.

EXERCISES

1. Taking your own clinical setting, look at the possibilities for ensuring privacy during interviews. Then look at your own workload and at the number of patients that you have to assess, and set a realistic time for any one assessment interview.

   a. Do your patients have a choice of where they are interviewed? If so, is this choice always available for them?

   b. What time did you put down as reasonable for an assessment interview? How does this match with the average length of interview that you have with a patient?

   c. What mechanisms do you have to make sure that assessment interviews are uninterrupted by the telephone, other staff or visitors?

   d. List three things that would help you to prepare more effectively for uninterrupted assessment of patients.

2. Return to Exercise 2 at the end of Chapter 1. Is your list of 'barriers' any different?

3

Setting the agenda

When trying to identify patients' problems, we have to remember that these come under a number of headings. We need to know, for example, what the physical problem is and what effect it has had on the patient's social life, and what other psychological problems may present, whether associated with the current physical situation or quite separate from it. We may have particular questions that we want to ask that will give us the detail necessary to plan the patient's care, but it is important at the end of the day that our assessment gives us a clear and accurate view of what is wrong with the patient in all three dimensions and how this is affecting that patient's day-to-day activities.

The patient's agenda

Traditionally, doctors, nurses and other health care workers have approached patients with a set of questions to which they need the answers. This is perfectly legitimate because they want to know what is wrong with the patient and what treatment or care is required. But if an interaction with the patient is to be truly effective, the answers to questions should be very much rooted in what the patient thinks and believes. What sort of priority the patient puts onto his problems may be very different from the picture that we would gain using a tick-list approach to assessment. In order to address all aspects of the patient's well-being, we must be willing to follow, to a reasonable degree, his own agenda of concerns. In this respect our assessment should be 'patient-led'.

Knowledge

It is important to find out what the patient's knowledge is of his current situation. It is normally reasonable to assume that the patient will know something about what is wrong with him. He may also have some idea of what is going to happen, but his actual knowledge may be very short of the reality. The following interaction demonstrates this:

> Doctor: Well, Mr West, can you tell me what the problem is?
>
> Mr West: Well, doctor, I wondered if you could give me a tonic; I'm tired and — I don't know — just not myself. I just don't know what the problem is, but I've got to pull myself together.
>
> Doctor: Can you tell me exactly what's making you feel that things aren't right?
>
> Mr West: Well, it's silly. I keep waking up in the night wanting a drink, and then of course, when I've had a drink I've got to go to the loo and I just seem to spend all night drinking and going to the toilet and it's because I can't sleep, you see.

In this sequence, Mr West understands that he has a problem, but obviously has not realized that it is unusual for somebody to be thirsty during the night or indeed to spend a lot of time going to the toilet. The doctor will be able to investigate the matter further and make a diagnosis; he will then, of course, need to explain to Mr West what the real problem is. Some patients are more articulate than Mr West, but even those who find it difficult to string words together feel more comfortable if they are allowed to describe their problem in their own words from their own perspective.

Sometimes it is easy to underestimate the patient's knowledge. When someone becomes ill or begins to feel that he has problems that are getting in the way of day-to-day activities, he will try to think why he has these problems and consider them in the light of his own knowledge and past experience. He may, for example, be able to identify a hereditary factor. By following the patient-led agenda in terms of finding out what he already knows about his illness, such problems can be more readily identified than by using a medically orientated check-list. Many nursing process forms and medical interview forms are based on a tick-list and tend to confine the information about the patient and his problems.

Belief

What a patient believes about his problems is probably as important as what he knows at a logical level. By exploring the patient's beliefs, it is often possible to understand particular responses to disease. For example, there are many myths and misconceptions about cancer. By allowing a patient to tell his story in his own words, it is possible to pick up on misperceptions and myths and have some chance of correcting them.

Mrs Jackson had breast cancer. She believed that she had caught it by helping a neighbour clear out a cellar after the neighbour's husband had died. She was convinced that cancer could be caught from a dirty environment where the previous occupant had cancer. This belief was important in terms of identifying problems because the patient was now convinced that she must not have any more to do with her neighbour in case her cancer recurred.

Often a patient's knowledge and belief about his particular situation can cause reactions that are difficult to understand unless one knows the cause. John Rogers was 40 and in good health; he jogged every day, worried about his diet and then, unexpectedly, had a coronary attack. The nurses who were caring for him sensed his anger but didn't realize in what it was based. In fact, John felt cheated. He believed that only people who were self-indulgent had heart attacks; because he felt that he had put a lot of effort into being healthy, he was convinced that he had unfairly drawn a 'short straw' and this made him extremely angry. One could have argued that his emotions would not get in the way of his treatment, but in fact they did because until his anger had been identified and defused his recovery was impeded.

Perspectives

The patient's perspective on his illness may be very different from that of the health professional. Indeed, it may be very different from that of his family, too. So it is important in a patient-led agenda that the perspective of the individual concerned is identified. The professional perspective will almost certainly be to identify actual problems, to plan care, set goals and evaluate whether those goals have been met. The individual's perspective might be quite different.

Elsie Mayes had been admitted with a lump in her breast for a two-stage operation and knew that she would have a mastectomy if her lump was found malignant. Mrs Mayes' perspective on the situation was rather different from that of the consultant. She pointed out that she did not want to go to theatre not knowing whether she would have a breast or not when she came back. She refused point blank to have a two-stage operation and explained that she would be quite happy to have the biopsy and then, if necessary, come back for the mastectomy. The consultant accepted that this was the only way that was acceptable to Mrs. Mayes. In this acceptance, the consultant was acknowledging that everybody is different and that what is seen to be most cost-effective and useful strategy for treatment is not acceptable to every patient. Only with effective interaction is it possible to identify the patient's perspective and accept that it is in fact a professional problem if the patient will not concur with the options that are offered.

Priorities

One of the stronger arguments for following a patient-led agenda in order to identify problems is that this enables the patient to feel free to set priorities. So often, a medical or nursing interview is based on a series of questions following a particular format. These are usually heavily weighted towards physical problems with very little emphasis on social or psychological concerns.

By asking patients open questions (see p. 29) the interviewer makes it possible for the patient to start his story where it is important to him and to talk about things that are of concern to him. For example, Mr West, who goes to his general practitioner because he is worried about not sleeping seems less anxious about his frequent trips to the lavatory. In this situation, the doctor will have to point out that by dealing with the diabetes that is causing the problem his sleep should improve.

Sometimes, however, priorities are more difficult for the health professional to understand. Faulkner (1985) describes a patient who was identified as a diabetic while in hospital for a small investigation. The patient acknowledged the diagnosis, but pointed out that she could not stay in hospital to be stabilized because she had promised her small daughter that she would be home on a certain day. Her priority was to maintain some trust between herself and her child. The consultant had to accept that priority and arrange for a day for the patient to come back into hospital to have treatment. If the patient's priorities are overridden, there is likely to be less compliance with the care that is prescribed.

The professional agenda

No matter how the interview is structured, one has to have a clear picture of the patient's current concerns in order to plan care. One argument against a patient-led agenda is that in fact vital information will be left undisclosed. The patient will talk about those affairs that are of concern to him and may not mention areas important to the health professional. In fact, if the patient is given the lead and is allowed to tell his story in his own way, he will normally cover most areas that the professional needs to investigate. If this turns out not to be the case, then it is possible for the professional to impose her own agenda to uncover the rest of the story, or to gain a more explicit account in order to make decisions on patient care.

Unfinished business

It may be that a patient has given a clear, coherent account of his current problems and any associated concerns, yet still has not given information that the professional needs in order to plan care. The professional can then clear up unfinished business at the end of the interview by referring to her own professional agenda. For example:

Nurse: Mr West, now that I've got a clear picture of the problems that you've been experiencing, I wonder if I can ask you a few specific questions that will help me to plan your care.

Mr West: Sure, anything else you want to know.

Nurse: Well, I wonder if you can tell me what your sleep pattern was like before this illness that you've been describing to me.

Mr West: Well, I always used to have a couple of tots, go to bed about 11 I suppose, sleep like a baby till the alarm went off in the morning.

Nurse: (laughing) So nothing much disturbed your slumbers?

Mr West: No, that's what's so worrying — it's just getting me down.

Nurse: Well, yes, I do understand that. You say you used to have a couple of tots before you went to bed — can you tell me a little bit about what you were drinking.

Mr West: Well, I'm not a big drinker myself, don't go into all that fancy stuff with wine and meals and that sort of thing, but I do like me pint and in the evening, just before I go to bed, I usually have a whisky.

Nurse: Well, so you don't like wine?

Mr West: No — beer and the occasional tot — that's all I ever have.

In her interview, the nurse gains from Mr West a clear idea of his newly acquired diabetes, the way in which he knew that something was wrong and a picture of his normal life pattern. He does not tell her about his normal sleep pattern nor yet about his alcohol consumption in his own account of his problems. These two items are cleared up without any difficulty. In following a patient-led agenda, the skill is in noting what has *not* been covered; in this instance, just two small but important items.

Sometimes unfinished business may be of a much more sensitive nature. Again, the nurse or doctor needs to use some skill in bringing these areas up for discussion. Subjects that patients do not always raise include partnership, social problems (particularly to do with finance) and problems which they believe may show them up in a bad light in some way. One can ask whether such topics should be raised if the patient is obviously avoiding them. In fact, things left unsaid can be as important as those that are said.

Let us go back to John Rogers, who was considerably angry following his heart attack, but who appeared to have few other major problems. Although he was known to be married, he had not mentioned his wife at all in his assessment interview. Staff talked to him soon after admission when he was feeling a little better rested and identified his current concerns. They picked up on his anger and gave him a chance to defuse it, but although they had the demographic detail that he was married, they realized that he had not mentioned his wife at all. By sensitively bringing up this area as an item of unfinished business during an assessment interview, a nurse learned that prior to John's heart attack his wife had in fact told him that their marriage was at an end and that she intended to live separately from him.

This information was important in that it certainly had implications for John's discharge and convalescence, but it also may have had something to do with John's current situation and his anger. At first sight, John's anger was all about having a heart attack when he had led a healthy life; in the course of further questioning it transpired that there was also quite a lot of anger directed towards his wife. John had seen himself as a perfect husband and breadwinner. He had thrown his energies into looking after the family concerns, paying the mortgage, paying the bills and putting the children into good schools, and he saw his wife's leaving him as an act of ingratitude.

John in fact needed counselling from a third party because he had not realized that what his wife wanted from life was a little different from what he was providing. She did understand his concern for their physical well-being; she did understand that he worked long hours; but what she did not understand was how these things could be more important than their emotional relationship. She had not confided in her husband that she often felt like a single parent because he was home late or working away. Consequently, anger had built up in her until a point when she was offered a very good job elsewhere.

The children were now old enough that she could see them in the holidays — they were away at school — and so she decided it was time to make a life for herself. By picking up on this area of unfinished business, the health professionals who were caring for John found no immediate solutions. They felt, however, that they understood a little more about his problems and were able to work with him to generate some plans for how he would deal with them.

Physical problems

Sometimes the professional has to go back to physical problems after the patient has completed his own agenda. Again, this should be simply a matter of alerting the patient to the fact that there are things that still need to be known in order that care can be coherently planned. In telling their stories, patients will often omit to talk of other illnesses — ones that they may have had or ones that are concurrent and for which they are receiving treatment. The health professional needs to know of these problems and needs to check again, as assessment continues, whether any of these areas have not been covered.

In the traditional interview, this question might be raised thus: 'Have you had any previous illnesses?' In a patient-led agenda it may be that when the patient is describing what is happening to him, the health professional will interject with a professional item: 'Have you had any other illnesses before this one, or was this the first time that you'd been ill enough to go to your doctor?' However, if this is seen to be intrusive and likely to stop the flow of the patient's disclosure, then it is best left to the end of the interview. The professional might say something like: 'Before I leave you, there's just one or two other things I need to ask you. You've given me a very clear history of your breast lump and what you've done since, but I wonder was that the first time you'd had any serious problems with your health?'

Patients do not appear to mind such questions being asked and tend to interpret them as a sign of interest: 'Not only did the doctor want to know about my lump and what's happened to me, but he wanted to know what's happened before. He was really interested in what I had to say.'

Some physical problems, of course, may have been deliberately omitted because the patient is embarrassed by them. These can include sexually transmitted diseases, previous abortions or accidents caused by physical abuse. Again, sensitive questioning should elicit disclosure of such problems, but in the final analysis the patient will reveal what he is able and not what is forced from him. The patient has the right to hold back information if it is too painful to discuss.

Psychological problems

Many illnesses engender psychological problems or indeed may result in psychological morbidity. It is important to check this out if there are any indications at all from the patient that this is the case. It is often extraordinarily difficult for someone to come to grips with the knowledge that he has a chronic or disabling disease. There is good evidence, for example, that patients who are given a diagnosis of cancer often react with anxiety and some indeed may become clinically depressed. Those patients with a terminal illness may have enormous difficulty in coming to grips with that sort of reality — indeed, many may not manage to do so.

In each of these situations, it is very unlikely that the patient will make his feelings explicit without some help from a professional. What he may do is to give some indication as to the way that he is feeling. This is a time when the health professional needs to move into a professional agenda — either taking her cue from the first or second hint or, at a later time, going back to what was said earlier. Let us stay with John Rogers:

Nurse: You say your wife is leaving. How do you feel about that?

John: I can't get it out of my mind — it goes round and round all the time: 'How am I going to cope — what will happen to her?'

Nurse: You say it's on your mind all the time.

John: Oh yes, it is more important at the moment than getting over this business of my heart.

Nurse: I'd like to come back to that later.

The nurse's response here is to become alert to the fact that John cannot distract himself from his grief over his wife leaving him. She obviously feels that it is an inappropriate time to go through the other symptoms of depression, and so she will need to ask some screening questions to elicit other symptoms such as mood change, sleep disturbance, weight and eating patterns, and interest in other pursuits.

Sometimes the professional agenda must be interjected into the actual interview itself. This may be because the cue that is given is so important. For example:

Patient: Sometimes, Doctor, I feel that the outlook is so grim I just wish I was dead and it was all over.

Here, the patient has given a hint of suicidal thoughts which obviously cannot be ignored. The doctor interviewing him should move into a professional agenda where he explores the pa-

tient's ideas about dying and should also screen for other signs of psychiatric morbidity. In picking up cues and moving into a professional agenda in this way, the health professional can acknowledge the importance of the disclosure and legitimize the patient's concern.

The rationale for this is that although the patient may feel safe enough to say he wonders if life is worth living, he may not give the other cues that the professional requires to make a judgement. For example, the patient who is waking early may not in any way connect that fact with changes in dietary habits, changes in mood or indeed with any other physical and psychological changes in his day-to-day living.

The professional agenda, then, complements the patient-led agenda. It allows the professional to raise important matters that may be missed by the patient, to pick up and amplify cues which may suggest other problems not disclosed by the patient, and to venture into sensitive areas which the patient may not feel able to address without help.

Patient-led
Story from patient's perspective
↓
Physical, social and psychological impact
↓
Interpretation of information
↓
Unanswered questions, fears and concerns

Professional items
Pick up cues, e.g. possible anxiety and/or depression. Cover areas omitted by patient.

Fig. 3.1 The interview agenda.

The need to negotiate

The fact that a patient presents himself at the ward, outpatient department, doctor's surgery or clinic does not mean that he has automatically put himself into professional hands without any let or hindrance. The patient remains an individual with thoughts, feelings and concerns and with a definite right to be involved in his own care. And even though some patients do not wish to have this level of involvement and are quite prepared to hand themselves over to health professionals, any interaction with a patient should be negotiated as far as possible.

Timing

There are many factors which affect the timing of an assessment interview. Obviously, if the patient is admitted as an emergency, then immediate medical action has to be taken and it will be later, when the patient is beginning to feel a little better, that anything more than the bare bones of the information required will be requested. A patient admitted for cold surgery may seem to be in a very different position and one could argue that the assessment interview could take place fairly soon after admission.

Patients are often quite stressed, even when coming in for simple surgery, and may need quite a while to settle down before they are able to talk through their concerns with the health professional. In Chapter 1, it was seen that when Joanna Hope was admitted the nurse asked her if it was convenient to ask her a few questions. This sort of negotiation allows the patient to know that the nurse is concerned about her and does not assume that she is immediately willing to answer any questions. In reality, few patients will say no, but there is always the possibility that they might and they do have a right to say, 'Sorry, nurse, I'm just not feeling like it at the moment, could it possibly be later?'

The difficulty is, of course, that when a nurse is sent to do an assessment interview on a patient and then the patient does not feel like talking, the nurse then has to reorganize her time so that she can come back later. What is important here is that the nurse negotiates with the patient, as in the following example:

Nurse:	Hello, Joanna. I wonder if I can ask you a few questions now so that we can properly plan your care?
Joanna:	Does it have to be now, Nurse?
Nurse:	Sounds as if you don't want to talk just now.
Joanna:	I'd rather not. I'm trying to sort

out something in my mind. I don't know that I would concentrate.

Nurse:	OK. I'll leave you now. Can I come back later, maybe after tea this afternoon?
Joanna:	Yes, yes. I'll talk now if you want me to.
Nurse:	No. I can see that you're distracted. Perhaps you'd want to tell me about that, too, but that's entirely up to you.

In this above exchange, the nurse has given Joanna the opportunity to say that she is trying to sort something out. She has obviously got a particular problem on her mind. The temptation is to go in and say, 'I can see you've got a problem — tell me what it is.' Here, negotiation is very important and Joanna made it quite clear that she wanted to deal with her thoughts alone. The nurse left the door open for a future discussion without any threat on either side.

Length of interview

The length of an interview certainly is not written in stone, but it does need to be negotiated with the patient so that both parties are quite clear on the parameters of the assessment. The notion that one has all the time in the world for the patient (see p. 10) is not to be encouraged, for two reasons:

1. It educates the patient to believe that he can avail himself of endless time
2. It gives the patient no incentive to prioritize worries and concerns.

If a definite time is negotiated, say 20 minutes to half an hour, then the patient has a chance to organize what he wants to say in that time. In fact, 20 minutes is quite a long time and allows an enormous amount of information to be exchanged.

In negotiating the length of an interview, the patient does, of course, have the right to question the proposed timing; the patient may feel the allotted time is too short or indeed too long:

Nurse: Joanna, I wonder if it's OK to ask you a few questions now?

Joanna: Yes, that's fine. You said you'd come back after tea.

Nurse: I think it'll take about 20 minutes and then we'll see how we go.

Joanna: But I'm not sure you'll be interested in me for 20 minutes.

Nurse: Well, let's see how it goes — it may not take that long.

In the above sequence, Joanna was assuming that all that would be talked about was her physical condition and she felt that there wasn't very much that would be necessary to say. The nurse, however, was interested in covering other areas too, and in fact 20 minutes was not quite long enough.

The negotiated duration for an interview can only be approximate. If one negotiates for 20 minutes, for example, this does not mean that at 20 minutes one stops short even though the interview is nearly complete. It may go on for another few minutes, but that is a very different matter from planning for 20 minutes and still being with the patient an hour later.

Some patients may feel that what they have to say is going to take considerably longer than the time prescribed by the health professional. In this instance, it may be that the health professional needs to renegotiate. For example:

Doctor: I need to talk to you, Mr Smith, before you have your operation.

Mr Smith: That's OK — I don't know what you need to know.

Doctor: Well, we need to find out about you and how you're reacting to the operation that you're going to have. I guess we'll need about 20 minutes for this.

Mr Smith: If you're really interested in me, you might as well go away again. The way I feel about this operation 20 minutes isn't going to touch it.

Doctor: I'm sorry about that, Mr Smith, but I wonder what we should do. Shall we start and see how far we can get and then if you do need more time, I can arrange to come back for another day?

Mr Smith: Why not today?

Doctor: Well, I've got six patients for theatre tomorrow and I want to get round them all and I won't do that if I don't ration my time.

Mr Smith: Sorry, Doctor, sorry. All right, let's start now, let's start now.

In the above sequence, Mr Smith's fear of his forthcoming operation is getting in the way so that he doubts whether the doctor will elicit the information he feels to be important in the time that is offered. The doctor, in negotiating a different time, and in explaining the constraints on his time at the moment, convinces Mr Smith that it is better to say what can be said in 20 minutes than to leave the matter altogether. The length of interview, then, needs to be negotiated with the patient, but within the reality of what the health professional can manage.

Note-taking

Many health professionals would argue that taking notes is not a good thing to do. They believe that it distracts the patient, gives the impression that there is less interest in the patient than in what is being written down, and gets in the way of proper interaction between patient and professional.

In fact, the reverse is true. By taking notes, one signals that what the patient is saying is so important that it must not be forgotten. The question then arises as to how one can both take notes and maintain interest in what the patient is saying. The most efficient way to take notes is indeed just to jot down headings. Figure 3.2 shows a nurse's headings in assessing a patient. It can be seen that the headings on their own would be fairly meaningless to anyone else, but they will allow the nurse to write an accurate history of the patient's concerns following the interview. By noting headings in this way, the nurse is able to give the patient the very real feeling that she is maintaining interest. She does

```
Mrs Hope
Admitted  20.10.91
Op.  Hysterectomy

Assessment
Heavy periods 6/12
Flooding
Dr - Consultant
Agreed op 1½ ago  Worry - away from home
Married ? problems .  Avoiding
Sons  5, 7.

On admission -
     Major   - boys' welfare ?
     Husband - ? not trust
                    selfish
Pt - in balance  re op
Other  problems - not ready to talk
Agreed  talk  again  after  op
```

Fig. 3.2 Note-taking using headings.

not have to look at the paper all the time, but can maintain reasonable eye contact.

Note-taking needs to be negotiated with the patient. The patient may be a bit alarmed at things being written down and, indeed, when talking about emotionally loaded areas may ask that notes are not taken. The health professional needs then to explain to the patient the purpose of note-taking, i.e. that by noting down the headings of the areas that have been covered, no facts that need to be known about the patient will be omitted.

Some health professionals prefer to use a small tape-recorder when interviewing patients. This can be quite unobtrusive and allows the whole history to be accurately recorded. It does, however, require transcribing afterwards so that all details can be noted. For the average interview, note-taking in the form of brief headings is probably the most efficient method in that it allows the nurse to write a history of the patient when she has more time.

If a patient objects violently to notes being taken, then one must desist, but it is worth point-ing out to that patient that it may not be possible then to remember all the details of the interview.

Confidentiality

When patients object to note-taking it is very often because they are concerned about confidentiality. Telling a nurse or a doctor problems and concerns may be very useful to the patient, but he may feel very differently if he thinks that other people may then read about him and know what his problems are.

This often results in patients requesting that certain information is not divulged to others. It is very seductive to have a patient say something along the lines, 'Nurse, I feel I can tell you what's on my mind, but I haven't been able to tell anybody else. Can you promise me that it won't go any further?' In fact, it is impossible to give such a promise for most concerns. This may sound hard, but if one is pressed to receive information that may not be divulged to anyone else, this information has to be refused. Consider the following exchange:

Mr Pepper: Nurse, you've been so understanding, I want to tell you something. I feel I can trust you, but I don't want it to go any further.

Nurse: I'm sorry, Mr Pepper, but I'm part of a team and I have to be free to discuss your problems with other team members; that's the only way we can make sure that your care is properly planned and carried out.

Mr Pepper: But it's very personal, Nurse.

Nurse: Well, I'll try and help you if I can, but I cannot be constrained. Obviously, if it's something that isn't relevant to your care, then it's a different story.

Mr Pepper: It would explain a lot of what I've been talking about.

Nurse: Well, it's really up to you.

Mr Pepper: But you won't talk about it, you definitely won't talk about it?

Nurse: No, but if it's relevant, it will go in your notes and it will be discussed within the team, but not outside this ward, obviously.

In the above exchange, the nurse is putting limits on what confidences she can accept and what she must be able to do with them. Many patients are concerned about disclosing confidential information because they have heard of nurses discussing patients on the bus. Obviously, such behaviour is very unethical and nurses can reassure patients on this point. What they must not do is to accept a confidence without being given the freedom to share it with the team.

Summary

In this chapter, the agenda of an assessment interview covering the physical, social and psychological concerns of the patient has been considered. It has been seen that a patient-led agenda will give a clear picture of the current situation from the patient's point of view. The areas that a patient may not cover that are important to the health professional can be covered by a professional agenda, either interspersed with the patient's agenda or at the end of it. Throughout the interview, there is the need to negotiate with regard to the timing and length of the interview, taking notes and confidential matters.

REFERENCE

Faulkner A 1985 Nursing: a creative approach: Baillière Tindall, London

---

EXERCISES

1. Choose a patient to interview with whom you feel comfortable. Follow a patient-led agenda, and negotiate over note-taking.

    a. Which areas of concern to you were not covered by the patient?

    b. What were the patient's main concerns?

    c. What effect did note-taking have on the interview?

2. When you next interview a patient, set a reasonable time limit with him.

    a. Did the patient appear to object to the time limit?

    b. How did the time limit affect the interview?

4

The skills of interviewing

There is no doubt that interviewing patients requires skills. These are often described as 'social skills' and from this comes the belief that they do not need to be learnt, since everyone develops social skills in their day-to-day interactions.

In fact, professional interactive skills are very different from social skills in several respects, not least of which are the subject matter covered and the (often) perceived difference in status between the patient, who may be seen as dependent, and the health professional, who may be seen as 'expert' and powerful, with the right to impose sanctions for non-compliance.

Certainly, the skills used in interviewing can also be useful in social interaction but one only has to eavesdrop on a bus or in a restaurant to realize that most social interaction is far from skilled and that those who are skilled are highly prized since they tend to be 'good listeners' and empathetic. The following conversation took place in the coffee shop of a well-known hotel:

Woman 1: It's lovely to see you again, Joan. How have things been with you?

Joan: Not good — it's Harry — I said to him the other day I might as well not have a husband — all I see of him.

Woman 1: They're devils, aren't they? John is just the same — late at the office — treats the house like a hotel.

Joan: I begin to wonder if there is another woman?

Woman 1:   Do you know, last week I asked him if he couldn't try to be home in time to have dinner with the family and he laughed — said if he didn't work hard there would be no dinner.

In this interaction, each woman was absorbed in her own story and almost competitive in wanting to describe the worse burden. Many individuals operate on this superficial level and would consider it prying to explore each other's concerns.

The health professional is concerned to encourage the patient to discuss concerns and feelings, and although some level of disclosure on the part of the professional may help this, the emphasis is not on the professional's concerns and feelings. The key skills required for effective interaction are as follows:

Openings

The way in which an interview starts is very important, particularly to someone who is coming to terms with changes in his life due to disease or disability. This is also true for relatives who are facing uncertainty and are deeply concerned for someone close to them or for whom they feel responsible. They need to know who the professional is, why he or she is there and why a wide range of questions are being asked which may seem unrelated to the current situation. As Fred, a postman in hospital for attention to his bunions, said: 'What the hell has my nightly tot of whisky got to do with my bunions!'

Consider the following openings with Elsie Mayes, who has been admitted for a mastectomy.

(1)

Nurse: Hello, Mrs Mayes. I need to ask you some questions.
Mrs Mayes: (puzzled) Yes?
Nurse: You know why you are here?
Mrs Mayes: Yes — it's this lump.
Nurse: Well, your breast — you will be glad to have it sorted.

(2)

Nurse: Hello, you are Mrs Mayes?
Mrs Mayes: That's right.
Nurse: I'm May Brown, the staff nurse, and I wondered if you feel ready for a chat. If we know something about you it helps us to plan the right sort of care.
Mrs Mayes: There isn't much to know (grins) but I'm happy to talk.
Nurse: Thank you. I guess this will take about 20 minutes, and I'd like to jot down a few notes so that I don't forget things.
Mrs Mayes: That's OK.

In (1), the nurse is concerned to get a history from the patient and overlooks the fact that Mrs Mayes may not have understood the object of the exercise. As a result, the patient is puzzled and confused. In (2), the nurse introduces herself clearly and negotiates the terms of the interview. This approach is more likely to generate trust and to lead to an accurate account of where the patient 'is at'.

Occasionally, a patient may be so nervous that even a negotiated opening may not bring results. If this happens it is important to acknowledge and explore this before proceeding with the interview:

Nurse: Hello, you are Elsie Mayes.
Mrs Mayes: (nods)
Nurse: I'm May Brown, the staff nurse, and I wondered if you feel ready for a chat. If we know something about you it helps us to plan the right sort of care.
Mrs Mayes: (no reply)
Nurse: Mrs Mayes?
Mrs Mayes: Go on — ask your questions.
Nurse: I get the feeling that you don't really want to talk. Can you bear to tell me why?
Mrs Mayes: (angrily) There isn't anything to talk about is there? My mother died at 35 — breast cancer. I've got breast cancer and I'm 35. End of story (starts crying).

In this sequence, the patient is consumed by the belief that she will die. The nurse has to explore this sensitively before proceeding with the more general interview.

Openings are normally made at a superficial level but if a patient discloses a serious concern, the level of interaction can become deeper very quickly in the hands of a skilled nurse (see Ch. 6). If the nurse feels that the levels are changing too quickly for the patient's emotional safety she can come back to the painful area later but she should make it clear to the patient that the matter will be addressed:

> Nurse: I can see that you are really worried about the possibility of dying. If I may I'd like to come back to that later, but first I'd like to know a bit more about you. Can you tell me how this all started?

The important thing here is that the distressing concern should be returned to, when the patient feels more able to discuss her feelings, and explored after further negotiation, e.g.:

> Nurse: You said at the beginning that you thought you would die like your mother — can you bear to tell me some more about that?

Questioning

When the terms of the interview have been negotiated with the patient, the questions required should be asked in such a way that the patient feels able to be open in his reply. There are three main types of questions: open, closed and leading.

Open questions

An open question is one that does not restrict the respondent in any way. In the sequence above the nurse says to Mrs Mayes, 'Can you tell me how this all started?' This is a good example of an open question: it gives the control to the patient, who can start her account at any time in the past that she considers significant.

Open questions also allow the expression of feelings, as in 'How did you feel when you found the lump?', and further exploration of those feelings, e.g. 'Can you tell me why you felt so worried?'

The important point about open questions is that no assumptions are made about the patient's perception of his current illness, or about his reactions to it.

Closed questions

Closed questions are those which give the respondent a forced choice of answer. They have been viewed with disfavour by many writers on communication, but they do have a place in interaction with patients where facts are required. Asking an individual how he feels about his home will not elicit information about his address. If such demographic data is required a closed question is most appropriate, e.g. 'Where do you live, Mrs Mayes?' The possible responses here are restricted to the actual address, refusal to give the address, or ignorance (however unlikely) of the address.

Even more restricted 'closed' questions are those that allow only a 'yes', 'no' or 'not sure' type of answer. Again, these may be appropriate for facts but not for knowledge of feelings, as is demonstrated by the following examples:

(1)

> Doctor: I see from the letter from your GP that you are about to retire. Is that correct?
>
> Patient: Yes, Doctor.

(2)

> Nurse: Do you understand why you are here?
>
> Patient: Yes.

(3)

> Doctor: Did you feel that things were going wrong at this time?
>
> Patient: Yes.

In each of these examples, the health professional can record a positive answer, but this will have limited value except in (1), where the closed question is used to check facts; even here, further open questions will be necessary to find the relevance (if any) of the impending retirement on the patient's current situation.

In (2) the nurse has not really gained any important information except that the patient *thinks* she knows why she is in hospital. In (3), the patient's response indicates concern but gives no more than a clue to his feelings and reactions. Open questions would have been more revealing, as in the following examples:

Nurse: Can you tell me what has brought you to hospital?

Patient: It's my gall bladder — I've had so much trouble, the doctor says I have to have stones removed.

Doctor: What did you think was the matter at this time?

Patient: Well, I thought something must be wrong — suddenly I was thirsty all the time and of course that meant I was trotting to the loo all the time.

It can be seen that closed questions restrict responses but are useful for facts and for checking available information.

Leading questions

Leading questions are those which imply the preferred answer, and as such are inappropriate in effective interaction, particularly since patients and their relatives tend to wish to please the health professional and give the 'correct' answer. Examples of leading questions are:

Hello, Mr Smith, I bet you are ready for a bath aren't you?
Well, Joanna, I'm sure you will be glad to get home, won't you?
Weren't you relieved when you knew we had a bed at the hospice?

In these examples, the expected response is clear. It is a brave patient who will disagree, even though his or her own ideas may be different. Mr Smith may hate the idea of a bath, Joanna may dread going home to her violent husband

Table 4.1   Three major types of questions

Question type	Effect	Example
Open (broad)	Control with respondent; allows disclosure	Well, Mr Brown, what has brought you here today?
Open (focused)	Control with respondent within a given area; encourages disclosure of feelings	How did you feel when you knew that your husband wouldn't recover?
Closed	Control with interviewer; extracts information or resistance or ignorance	What is your date of birth?
Closed (forced choice)	Control with interviewer; checks information	You say you fear heights Is that why you live in a bungalow?
Leading	Control with interviewer; suggests desired response	You would enjoy having your hair washed, wouldn't you?

and the patient who is terminally ill may have very mixed feelings about admission to the hospice.

Leading questions should not be confused with focused open questions. In the examples on page 29 a broad open question was used: 'Can you tell me how this all started?' Later, more focused questions may be used but they should remain open, e.g. 'You say you can't sleep. What do you think about when you are awake?' Here the patient has control over her response and is not led in any way. A leading question makes assumptions, as in: 'You say you can't sleep. I'll bet you are worrying about this operation, aren't you?'

Table 4.1 summarizes the three main types of questions.

Facilitation

The previous sections may give the impression

that, if the interview is negotiated and open questions are asked, patients and relatives will willingly disclose their problems and feelings about their history and current situation. The reality is rather different, since this may be the first time that an individual has had the opportunity to explore areas which are socially taboo. To overcome such barriers, the health professional requires the skill of facilitation, i.e. the ability to overcome obstacles and to make it easier for the patient to verbalize concerns. Consider the following interaction between a nurse and George, who has recently been bereaved but is controlling his emotions rather than giving way to his grief.

Nurse: You say it is 8 weeks since your wife died. Can you bear to tell me what it was like at the time she died?

George: I coped. Everyone said how well I coped.

Nurse: (gently) But how did you feel?

George: I coped. That's me, I put the lid on.

Nurse: But you?

George: A bloody nightmare — I couldn't believe she wasn't breathing anymore.

Nurse: And afterwards?

George: I went through the motions — it's a haze now — everyone kept saying I was brave.

Nurse: I guess it's still difficult to talk about?

George: But I shouldn't worry you about it.

Nurse: If you can bear to talk, I will listen. It might help.

In this interaction the nurse is facilitative in that she acknowledges the problem and makes it legitimate. She then shows her willingness to share George's painful feelings.

Two other attributes help to facilitate disclosure; one is empathy; the other is the ability to make educated guesses (sometimes called understanding hypotheses) from the information already given.

Empathy

There are many definitions of 'empathy', including the ability to get inside another's skin so that perfect understanding of his or her feelings is possible. In fact, each individual's reactions are different and it is not possible to know precisely what it feels like to be a particular individual in a particular situation, especially if his or her experience has not been part of one's own life experience. What *is* possible is to build a picture from an individual's disclosures so that one can begin to understand these reactions. Empathetic responses then come almost naturally (Faulkner 1984).

Because of the uniqueness of each individual's feelings and reactions, a patient may well doubt a health professional's ability to empathize, especially if that professional is young. The following vignettes show two approaches to such a reaction.

(1)

Nurse: I think I can begin to understand how devastated you must feel after the death of your wife.

George: Understand? A chit of a girl like you. What have you ever lost? How *can* you understand?

Nurse: Please help me to understand.

George: It's like losing part of myself.

(2)

Nurse: I understand how devastated you must feel after the death of your wife.

George: Understand? A chit of a girl like you? How can you understand?

Nurse: I know I'm young, but I meet a lot of people like you.

In (1) the nurse acknowledges that she needs help to understand and therefore comes across as empathetic and willing to listen, whereas in (2) the nurse attempts to 'normalize' George's pain and so appears to lack both empathy and understanding.

Educated guesses

A more formal definition for an educated guess

is 'making an understanding hypothesis'. In practice this means collating information that has been given so that realistic guesses can be made about the overall effect of the current situation on the patient. For example, Joanna Hope (p. 4) may describe her reactions to hysterectomy and disclose that there are potential problems in the weeks after discharge when she may not feel ready for a resumption of sexual activity. The health professional may feel, from the information available, that Joanna is nervous about her husband and his ability to understand the problem. An educated guess could be: 'From what you are saying, I get the feeling that your husband may not understand that it will be a while before you feel able to resume sexual activity.'

Many professionals feel very nervous about making such guesses, fearing that if they have 'got it wrong', the patient will fail to respond. In fact there are several ways in which an individual is likely to react to an educated guess. He or she may:

- agree
- agree and elaborate
- disagree
- disagree and elaborate.

Each of these types of response will be considered in turn.

Agree. In this case, Joanna may well respond with: 'Well, I don't think he will understand. Why should he?' It is then up to the health professional to explore further the patient's particular worries and to work with her to generate solutions.

Agree and elaborate. Here the patient feels safe enough not only to agree, but to give more information on the subject: 'No, I don't think he will understand. He will argue that I've been here [in hospital] for a while and that he has needs for me to fulfil. It was the same when Sammy, the baby was born. Only a few days — I was sore — but he insisted.' In this instance, Joanna is working on past experience in considering her problems.

Disagree. Sometimes, even with articulate information, educated guesses may be inaccurate.

Most patients will correct the health professional. For example, Joanna's response to the guess that she feels her husband may not understand her need for 'space' before resuming her sexual relationship, may be corrected: 'No, no, it isn't that he won't understand.' Here, Joanna is correcting the health professional but leaving it up to her to pursue the question further.

Disagree and elaborate. In this situation, Joanna will not only correct the health professional's impression but will also explain further: 'Oh no, it isn't that he won't understand — he won't **want** to understand — he's selfish in bed and not very gentle — I hate the thought of it.'

It can be seen that educated guesses can help to 'move a patient on' and that, even if the guess is incorrect, much may still be learned about a patient's concerns by putting information together to help complete the picture.

Checking one's guesses with the patient is essential; otherwise a quite erroneous picture may be built up by jumping to conclusions and making assumptions, as in the following exchange:

Nurse: From what you are saying, I get the feeling that your husband may not understand that it will be a while before you feel able to resume sexual activity.
Joanna: (pauses) Well . . .
Nurse: If he loves you, of course he won't want to wait.
Joanna: If only it were that simple.
Nurse: Now stop worrying, do, we will have a word with him.

Here, because the nurse does not allow Joanna to respond to her guess, the real worry about pain and violence is not aired.

The most important point to remember about educated guesses is that they should be based on what the *patient* communicates, not on the interviewer's own experiences or assumptions.

Cues

If a patient-led agenda is to be followed, it is

important to pick up the cues to concerns that are offered. Patients seldom ask direct questions but are more likely to give cues. Many authors suggest that a missed cue is a disaster. This is not so, for a patient will continue to offer important cues until they are accepted and explored, or until the patient picks up the message that his cues are not acceptable to the interviewer.

Let us return to the case of Mr Smith, who is afraid of dying under an anaesthetic. He may be aware at a logical level that his fear is irrational. This may prevent him from saying 'I've got this awful feeling I may die on the operating table' for fear that he will be laughed at. His fear, however, will remain and may only be identified if cues are picked up and explored:

Doctor:	Have you had an anaesthetic before, Mr Smith?
Mr Smith:	(nervously) No.
Doctor:	You don't sound too sure.
Mr Smith:	Well . . .
Doctor:	Do you want to tell me about it?
Mr Smith:	Oh, I shouldn't worry.
Doctor:	But you do?
Mr Smith:	Yes — I worry what if I don't wake up.

The cues here are the patient's nervousness and his allusion to worry. These could easily be missed:

Doctor:	Have you had an anaesthetic before, Mr Smith?
Mr Smith:	(nervously) No.
Doctor:	Nothing to it, you will wake up and find it's all over.
Mr Smith:	Oh, I shouldn't worry.
Doctor:	Of course not! You are in good hands here.

In the first example, Mr Smith is given the opportunity to explore his concerns. In the second, he is actively discouraged from explaining his concerns. Cues are often subtle, but by exploration we can gain a better perspective on a patient's fears and worries.

Precision

Often, when an individual is encouraged to give an account of his history, he may talk rather vaguely. This is often especially true with regard to time. It requires skill on the part of the interviewer to encourage precision so that an accurate picture can be gained.

Concern has sometimes been expressed that to 'pin someone down' in this way will cause irritation. In fact, the reverse appears to be true in that the patient or relative appreciates the opportunity to reflect and so gain insight into the current situation. Consider the following extracts from two interviews:

(1)

Nurse:	Can you tell me when this all started?
George:	Oh, it were a few months back.
Nurse:	And what happened?
George:	I had this pain.
Nurse:	And?
George:	Well, it kept me awake, like.

(2)

Nurse:	Can you take me back to the beginning, Ellen?
Ellen:	Well the first thing was feeling so tired.
Nurse:	When exactly was that?
Ellen:	After my holiday . . . July . . . the end of July. I thought it was going back to work.
Nurse:	So that was two months ago.
Ellen:	Yes, and then I was thirsty, always wanting a drink of water.

In the first abstract the information is unclear, but in the second the nurse encourages the patient to be precise. As does Ellen, most individuals can pin-point an occurrence by linking it with another event. In this case the other event was the end of a holiday; by remembering this, Ellen could identify the exact time she became worried about her health.

Clarification

Clarification complements precision in that it also helps to give an accurate picture from the patient's perspective. Clarification is required

Table 4.2   A 'normal' night's sleep

Name	Approx. bedtime	Rise time	Times awake approx.	Activities on a normal night
Mary	21.00	7.30	1	Just go back to sleep
Samuel	23.00	8.00	—	—
Penny	23.30	6.00	2	Go to loo
Matthew	2.00	7.00	—	—
Sarah	23.00	6.30	—	—
Peter	22.00	8.00	2	Lie awake/go to loo
Ann	21.00	5.30	1	Make a drink and read

when the patient uses an ambiguous word, of which there are many in our language. The general meaning of the word may be the same for everyone but the specific meaning may be different. Take the word 'normal', for example, and consider a 'normal' night's sleep. Table 4.2 gives examples of the wide range of meaning signified by the word 'normal'.

All of the individuals in Table 4.2 report a 'normal' night's sleep, but what they actually mean is 'normal for me' and any reported problems will be in relationship to that normality. From this it becomes clear that questions such as 'Do you eat a normal breakfast?' elicit little information compared to a question which clarifies, e.g. 'Please describe your usual sleep pattern' or 'Tell me what you usually eat for breakfast.'

Other words which need clarification are those for which there is both a social and professional meaning. These include 'depressed', 'diarrhoea' and many others. The word 'depression' when used by a patient may mean anything from sadness to clinical depression. The need to clarify here is important if the patient's needs are to be met, because clinical depression may need physical treatment before the patient is able to discuss and find solutions for other problems. Similarly with physical conditions. Many people think that diarrhoea means going to the toilet more frequently than is normal for them.

Control

If we think of patient-led agendas and identify-

ing problems, 'control' may seem an inappropriate term. Open questions, for example, give control of the topic to the patient. If a patient is asked 'How have things been for you?', he is free to explore physical, social or psychological issues. This allows the professional to build a picture of the patient's current concerns from *his* perspective. Permission to disclose in this way may be a new phenomenon to the patient, who may feel nervous of articulating concerns and may divert to less painful areas, as in the following example:

Nurse: Hello, Vera, how are things with you?
Vera: Not too good — it's the pain.
Nurse: Oh dear, can you tell me when it came back?
Vera: It was visiting time. Sarah came to see me with Mary. What a baby! Only ten months old and all over the place.
Nurse: I saw her here last week. She has gorgeous eyes.
Vera: Yes, and she is standing now — walking soon I guess.

In this sequence, the nurse is diverted from Vera's pain to her little grand-daughter. It takes sensitive control to keep Vera to the point while accepting her pride in the little girl:

Nurse: Hello, Vera, how are things with you?
Vera: Not too good — it's the pain.
Nurse: Oh dear, can you tell me when it came back?
Vera: It was visiting time. Sarah came to see me with Mary . . .
Nurse: (cutting in) Your lovely grand-daughter — I'd love to hear about her later, but can we come back to the pain?
Vera: It was when they left — I was a bit upset — and then the pain came.
Nurse: Can you tell how severe it was?
Vera: So severe, it took my breath away.

In this second sequence, Vera is kept to the point in such a way that she is not offended. Rather, she recognizes that the nurse is giving top priority to *her* and *her pain*.

Another situation when control is necessary is one in which the patient will not stop talking. When asked to give an account of the current situation, the patient repeats the same material, rather like a gramophone record that is stuck in a groove. Control can be exerted here by acknowledging the problem and attempting to 'move the patient on', e.g.:

Joanna:	. . . and there was another time — he didn't fancy his dinner — then he just threw it at me, I was *so* scared.
Doctor:	You have given many examples of your husband's violence — I guess you have bottled it up for a long time — but I wonder if we can talk now about any other concerns you have about going home?
Joanna:	It's mostly him.
Doctor:	I know that, but are there other worries?
Joanna:	Well I wonder how I will cope at home . . .
Doctor:	Any particular aspects?
Joanna:	Well . . . lifting, and driving the car — and managing the children.

Again, Joanna does not appear to mind the doctor exerting control, but she does have difficulty in moving away from the subject of her husband's violent behaviour. The doctor acknowledges the problem and in doing so, legitimizes the strain and worry.

Sequencing

Sequencing means, briefly, exhausting one topic before starting another, or before giving advice. Control is important here in keeping to the point and in avoiding repetition. If a sequence is not completed, inappropriate assumptions may be made and perhaps advice given which will not help in the particular situation. For this reason, the assessment should be complete before any advice is given.

In encouraging the patient to disclose her concerns, the interviewer should try to ensure a smooth movement from one sequence to another. This is usually effected with a 'transition statement', as in the following example:

Mr Smith:	. . . and that is why I am scared of dying.
Nurse:	I can see that, but I wonder if there are other reasons?
Mr Smith:	Only one silly one.
Nurse:	Silly?
Mr Smith:	Yes, a childhood nightmare that I was looking down on myself on the operating table and knowing I was dead.
Nurse:	How awful for you. And I wonder if you can tell me how these fears are affecting how you feel about the operation.
Mr Smith:	Sounds daft, but the operation doesn't worry me at all. I've had it explained to me and it seems OK.

In this exchange, the nurse uses a transition statement to move from the patient's fear of dying to his attitude towards the operation itself, after first acknowledging the awfulness of the fear and its manifestations.

Closing

In Chapter 2 the need to negotiate the timing and duration of an interview was considered. Many health professionals are encouraged to give the impression that they have 'all the time in the world'. Such an impression will make closing very difficult, especially if the patient or relative is lonely, or has had little opportunity to ventilate feelings. There are a number of closing strategies which will help to bring an interview to its end; these are described below.

Time reminder. If timing has been negotiated at the beginning of an interview, it is worthwhile to alert the patient a little before the time is up, e.g. 'I see we have about five minutes left, Mr Smith.' If time has *not* been negotiated, it is still useful to let the patient know that time is nearly up, e.g. 'I will have to bring this to a close in a few minutes.' Both of these statements remind the patient that time is finite and encourage him to prioritize remaining concerns.

Summarizing. It is useful to summarize from time to time in an interview, but particularly so when an interview is coming to an end. This allows the patient to confirm that the health professional has gained a clear understanding of his current concerns, or to correct any misunderstanding, as in the following example.

| Nurse: | Well, Mr Smith, it seems that your main concerns are to do with fears of dying on the operating table, and also of problems after discharge. You are happy about the operation itself. |
| Mr Smith: | Not *happy* exactly, but I feel I understand what is happening. |

In this example, the correction is one of degree, but it could equally be concerned with facts. A final summary is a cue to the fact that the interview is coming to a close.

Screening questions. A screening question is used to check that all important issues have been addressed. This may seem a strange item to include under the heading of 'closing', but it is important to leave the patient feeling that he has had the opportunity to disclose his major concerns. Occasionally a patient may see this as a chance to start a new dialogue; in this situation, the skills of control and negotiating need to be used sensitively, e.g.:

Nurse:	You say that I have correctly picked up on your problems. Can I ask if there is anything else?
Mr Smith:	You have been so understanding — I *do* have another problem but it's to do with my son.
Nurse:	But not about your operation?

Mr Smith:	No, oh no, it's a long story . . .
Nurse:	Well, I'd love to listen, but our time is nearly up. Perhaps I can arrange to talk to you again.
Mr Smith:	I'd appreciate that — it's *very* confidential.

The above sequence is possible because the nurse had negotiated the time, and is showing interest as well as exerting control.

Closing statements. The final closure of an interview should be made clear with an unambiguous statement. This may include a statement about the future or another time setting; alternatively, the final word may be left with the patient. It is then important to exert control in order to avoid re-openings, as in the following:

Nurse:	Well, I'll see you again on Wednesday . . .
Mr Smith:	Yes, and you said you would send the anaesthetist to talk to me.
Nurse:	That's right.
Mr Smith:	Will he be able to put my mind at rest? Will he understand?
Nurse:	I *do* know how anxious you are, but I think you should save your questions for him. Now I really must go, I'll pop back when I have an appointment for you.
Mr Smith:	Thank you — I know I'm an old fussbudget — I will try to be patient.
Nurse:	(kindly) It won't be long. 'Bye now.

In this sequence, Mr Smith makes a bid to hold the nurse back, but her gentle control allows her to leave.

Summary

In this chapter the verbal skills required for an effective interview have been considered. These include employing an appropriate questioning style, encouraging precision and clarification, picking up cues and at all times using a negotiating style which facilitates disclosure of current concerns. The need for control and skilled opening and closing strategies has been considered.

REFERENCE

Faulkner A 1984 Teaching non-specialist nurses assessment skills in the aftercare of mastectomy patients. Unpublished Ph D thesis, University of Manchester (Steinberg Collection, Royal College of Nursing)

EXERCISE

1. Read the following transcript of an interview. Look for examples of skills and the effect of their use.

   a. Pick *three* examples of open questions

   b. Find an example of a cue, and note how it was picked up

   c. Which skills were used in closing the interview?

   Transcript of an interview from 'Child of a Dying Patient', Help the Hospices, London (see Resources, p. 103).

Interviewer:	Rob, you're not usually here when I come to see Pam, but I'm glad you are because it gives me a chance to ask you how you're coping now?
Rob:	Well I'm coping. I've got a full-time job, looking after the children as much as I can so that she doesn't have to do too much. I'm coping.
Interviewer:	Yes. And we've talked before and it's obvious, although you've got a busy life, you are still fitting it all in. I just wondered if you were . . .
Rob:	You have to. You just can't stop.
Interviewer:	I know, but it must be quite tough.
Rob:	You don't have time to think about that, you just do it.
Interviewer:	OK. What about the boys?
Rob:	Well they're looked after as well as they can be. Pam can't do things for them that she used to do. She finds she can't stand up for more than 10 minutes at a time without getting tired and having to sit down, and so we bought a microwave. I can cook at the weekends and do individual dinners and she can whack 'em in the microwave for when the boys come home from school.
Interviewer:	But how are the boys taking this quite difficult situation?
Rob:	Well, they're not taking it any differently because they don't know she's dying.
Interviewer:	So you haven't levelled with them?
Rob:	No, they know she's ill, but that's it.
Interviewer:	And do you think they accept that?
Rob:	What, that she's ill?
Interviewer:	Mm.
Rob:	Yes, because she has to spend a lot of time in bed and when she's not able to take them, I take them to school before going to work. Obviously, things are different. Sometimes they go to school with friends who have also got children there, so they know she's ill and they must appreciate — although I've never stressed it — that she's very ill.

Interviewer:	Could you tell me why you haven't made it more explicit how ill she is?
Rob:	Yes, because she doesn't know.
Interviewer:	I see.
Rob:	She doesn't know she's dying. She thinks she will get over it. If I tell them, they will tell her — not necessarily go straight up and say 'Mum, Dad says you're dying' — but they will tell her in other ways, and I don't want her to know because as long as she doesn't know, she's got hope and if you take away that hope she will die very quickly.
Interviewer:	Mm. That's Pam, and I can see that does then cause problems for the boys, but I'm just wondering if there are other reasons why you haven't told them.
Rob:	No, but children can't keep a secret. If you take the average child and presumably the younger they are the more quickly it happens — you take something like Christmas. They go out and they buy you a present and it's a big secret — 'Oh don't tell Mum you've bought the present, keep it until Christmas' — within a very short while they've said, 'Oh I'm not allowed to tell you I've bought you an X, Y, Z.'
Interviewer:	They get excited.
Rob:	That's right, they get excited.
Interviewer:	I realize that.
Rob:	And if I was to tell the boys that Pam was dying they would, if they were able to keep a secret, they would show it by their extra concern for her. They'd go out and spend their pocket money on buying her something little every week and she'd soon know that they were being over-protective, if you like.
Interviewer:	It sounds as if you're trying to protect everybody on your own.
Rob:	I've got to protect Pam from finding out. It's the only time I've ever deceived her. I'm basically completely honest, but I haven't told her because I don't want her to know, and in order to protect Pam then, yes I have to shield it from the boys knowing, so therefore, I can't let them know. Apart from the specialist, the doctor and me, nobody knows. If that's shielding everybody then alright I'm shielding everybody, but it's not conscious. I want to shield her.
Interviewer:	I can understand that, but I wonder if you can think of any reasons why it might be a good idea for the boys to have some idea of the reality of the current situation?
Rob:	Well, they know she's very ill because sometimes she can't get out of bed and all the rest of it. Except for saying to them, 'Look, your mother is dying', I can't say to them — she's very ill, I told you yesterday she was ill and today she's very, very, very ill — there's not much elasticity in 'very ill'.
Interviewer:	Have they asked you any questions?
Rob:	They were told that she was very ill 18 months ago or 2 years ago when she first had it before she had the breast removed which was 18 months ago, and they know that she isn't getting any better. They can see she's not getting any better — she's lost a lot of weight — but I can't tell them how ill she is without telling them exactly how ill she is. So as far as they're concerned she's ill.

Interviewer: Yes. And are you saying that if they did ask questions, you'd feel unable . . .

Rob: No, when they ask questions they say, 'Is Mum any better today? Has Mum had a good day?' Or they say to her, 'How do you feel?' Those are the sort of questions they ask.

Interviewer: You haven't given me any good reasons why you think it might help to tell them — can you think of any?

Rob: Not really, because I don't believe that children can keep that sort of information to themselves. They might not say to her, 'Dad says you're dying.' They might say it to a friend of theirs at school and then she might go out and meet the mother of the friend and the friend might say, 'Well, you look good for somebody who's dying.' It would get back to her.

Interviewer: So your real concern, as you made clear earlier on, is Pam.

Rob: Yes, because while there's life, there's hope. As soon as she gives up hope, she'll give up life.

Interviewer: But have you thought about the situation after she has died as far as your children are concerned?

Rob: I haven't given it a great deal of thought, no. I tend to face that sort of thing as it happens.

Interviewer: Because sometimes, even though children don't come out with it, they make a lot more sense of a situation than we imagine.

Rob: I hope you're right, because if she does die then I might need them to make some sense of it.

Interviewer : Would you be prepared for me to talk to the children if they're prepared to talk to me — and not to tell them anything that you haven't told them, but simply to find out what sense they're making of the situation?

Rob: You've met them before, they know you. You can talk to them if you like, but you mustn't tell them that Pam is dying.

Interviewer: I promise you that I won't tell them that Pam is dying, but if they should let me know, that is if they are prepared to speak to me, that they are concerned about that, then obviously I 'd come back to you and apprise you of where they're at, but it might just help to free things up but you might be absolutely right — it might be that they are just taking each day as it comes. Thank you for saying that I can talk to them because it will give them a chance to say what's on their mind, if it's anything and if they are all right then, well, yes, OK. And sometime I would like to talk to you, though not today, about Pam and where she is at in this.

Rob: Well she doesn't believe that it's terminal.

Interviewer: No, OK — but I'd like to leave that for today. Perhaps we can have a talk after I've talked to the boys and see how we go from there. Is that OK?

Rob: Yes, you can talk to them certainly. It could be that you're right that they know more than I give them credit for — that since Pam doesn't know, and I haven't told them — there's been nothing mentioned in the house that she's that ill and normally children pick up what's going on around you — say something you don't want them to hear and they hear it.

Interviewer: They're usually very perceptive, aren't they?

Rob: They don't miss a lot. That sounds like one of them now.

5

Non-verbal interaction

The importance of non-verbal interaction in health care has been very well documented (e.g. Argyle 1988). It is certainly true that even when no words are spoken a picture of an individual can come across clearly from:

• body language
• style of dress
• stance
• facial expression.

Many first impressions are made on the basis of non-verbal signals, although it can be argued that non-verbal behaviour is unconscious and perhaps influenced by personality or mood at any given time. This can lead to the categorization of individuals on continua. For example, one individual may be described as warm and outgoing where someone else is described as cold, purely on the basis of non-verbal behaviour. Similarly, some individuals are considered to be empathetic while others are not, and whether or not empathetic words are spoken it is the non-verbal accompaniment to the response that is deemed to be important. Davis & Ternulf-Nyhlin (1982) found that a control group was seen to be more able to give realistic empathetic reassurance than an experimental group that had been taught about empathetic responses. Such findings suggest that non-verbal behaviour cannot be taught, but Faulkner (1984) found that as nurses' communication skills improved so did their empathetic and warm responses to the patients that they assessed.

The interrelationship between verbal and non-verbal behaviour

The separate consideration of verbal and non-verbal skills and behaviour in this chapter is for convenience rather than to represent the reality, where both verbal and non-verbal behaviour are closely interrelated. It has already been seen that a verbal empathetic response needs to be linked with empathetic behaviour if the message is to be believed. Similarly, if verbal facilitation and negotiation is undertaken in a cold, detached way then there is less likelihood that the patient will respond than if the interviewer is warm and facilitative.

An interesting dimension to this interrelatedness is that, in general, if concurrent verbal and non-verbal messages do not match, then the non-verbal message is the one more likely to be believed:

Nurse:	It sounds as if you are having a terrible time.
Joanna:	You're shocked, aren't you nurse?
Nurse:	No I'm not shocked, no, I just wonder how you put up with it.
Joanna:	You are shocked, I can see it in your face.

In this exchange the nurse listens to Joanna and reacts internally with shock and surprise that any woman could put up with the behaviour from a partner that Joanna is describing. Joanna correctly picks up the shock from the nurse's non-verbal behaviour. This poses a problem in real terms, for if health professionals are to be non-judgemental, caring, and able to listen to their patients' problems, then they may have to change certain attitudes and beliefs. The choice is to wear a mask so that one's true feelings are hidden, or to empathize and disclose true feelings and reactions.

In real life everyone wears a mask from time to time to hide feelings that are difficult to deal with. This is a natural defence mechanism, accepted as a normal aspect of social behaviour. The proper balance in health care lies in being able to show feelings and accept other people's reality without wearing a mask all the time. It is also sometimes appropriate to show shock, but then the verbal response should match the feeling. In Faulkner's study (1984), a young nurse, assessing a patient, heard that the patient's husband was not only having an affair but was bringing his girl-friend to the ward at visiting time. The patient was cross with her husband and asked the nurse if she felt that she was being unreasonable. The nurse was obviously shocked by the story and her response both verbally and non-verbally matched exactly, as she looked very angry and said 'Hard on him? *Hard* on him? I'd go for the b—— with a bread knife.' Obviously, that level of empathy has be contained in some way, but after that exchange the patient was much more able to be open with the nurse about her fears and concerns.

NON-VERBAL SKILLS

In the same way that there are verbal skills that need to be developed to improve interaction between health workers and patients, there are non-verbal skills that can be developed to further enhance interaction. This concept moves away from the belief that non-verbal behaviour is totally unconscious and a part of each individual, but argues rather that skilled use of non-verbal language can be very beneficial both to the individual and to the patient.

Listening

When two people are interacting, at any one time one will take the role of the talker while the other takes the role of the listener. What cannot be assumed is that the person taking the role of the listener *is* in fact listening to the other individual. Very often the 'listener' is waiting for a chance to talk again, and may not be concentrating very hard on what his companion is saying. It is therefore possible to divide listening into two broad categories: active listening and passive listening.

Active listening

In active listening there are clear indications that

the message coming across is being heard and responded to:

Mrs Mayes: Well when I found the lump I was just terrified.
Nurse: (nodding) Mmm.
Mrs Mayes: I'd always dreaded it, you see.
Nurse: Dreaded it?
Mrs Mayes: Yes, because of my mother, I suppose I'd always believed that if it could happen to her it could happen to me.
Nurse: Go on.

In this exchange the nurse demonstrates to Mrs Mayes that she is actively listening to her story. She encourages her to continue by saying 'Mmm' and nodding. She shows that she is taking in what the patient is saying by repeating key words. Active listening can also be demonstrated by non-verbal signs such as facial expressions and gestures.

Passive listening

In passive listening the 'listener' shows no sign of actually hearing the story that is being told. At worst she may look bored or indeed distracted and there is no sign that the specific words used have been heard:

Mrs Mayes: When I found the lump I was terrified.
Nurse: (no reaction)
Mrs Mayes: You see, well it was just awful.
Nurse: Have they told you which day you are going to have your operation?

In this exchange it is quite obvious that the nurse is not picking up on the fears that the patient is expressing. It may be that she is not listening for a number of reasons. These may include the blocking of an unpleasant message. The patient is very likely in these circumstances to become aware that her message is not being received and may become educated not to attempt to give that message again (see p. 33). Interactions will remain on a superficial level,

and the patient's real fears and concerns may not be identified at all.

During assessment, the balance of 'talk' puts the health professional in the major role of listener. By listening actively the professional will encourage patients to disclose their real fears and worries. Active listening also allows the interviewer to have control in an interaction, because by picking up key words and by encouraging disclosure, he or she will be able to note any diversion from the focus of the interaction. Passive listening, on the other hand, can encourage a 'gramophone record' interaction, as when a patient simply wants to tell his story over and over again without any depth or detail, very often losing the point of the interview.

Silence

The effective use of silence is a skill that can be developed, although in social interaction silence is often seen as failure and can be very uncomfortable, particularly between relative strangers. Most individuals have had the experience of being introduced to someone new and feeling totally tongue-tied. There is often no point of contact, or knowledge of the other person's interests, so that conversation may be limited to the weather, the latest sports results, or the latest happenings in the political world.

Silence can be used very constructively in an assessment interview. Questions that are asked are often difficult for the patient because they cover areas which are socially taboo. Patients may need to think about their responses, to organize their thoughts, and to articulate their worries or concerns. Too often the health professional will rush in with other questions, such that any important point that the patient may have wanted to discuss is lost forever. Consider the following examples:

(1)

Nurse: Can you tell me what is worrying you about this operation, Mr Smith?
Mr Smith: (pause)

Nurse: Is this the first time you have been in hospital?

Mr Smith: Well it is the first time I've been in for an operation.

Nurse: Well tell me what you know about the operation.

(2)

Nurse: Can you tell what is worrying you about this operation?

Mr Smith: (pause)

Nurse: (waits)

Mr Smith: Well it's a bit of a long story and it's to do with a pal of mine . . .

In the first exchange the nurse is uncomfortable with the silence and moves on to other questions, which in fact are easier for Mr Smith to answer. In the second exchange the nurse uses the silence to allow Mr Smith to sort out how he wants to respond.

The skill in using silence is in knowing how long to wait before making a further comment. If a silence goes on for too long then both individuals become uncomfortable and it then may be very difficult to take the interview any further. If a silence is over-long then one strategy is to acknowledge what is happening:

Nurse: Mr Waters, you've been looking after your wife for a long time, and I think you are very tired, I wonder if you would consider letting her come into the hospice?

Mr Waters: (pause)

Nurse: (waits)

Mr Waters: (continues in silence)

Nurse: Mr Waters, I get the impression that you're finding this a very difficult area to discuss.

Mr Waters: Yes, Nurse, I am. You are right that I am tired, but you see I promised her.

Here the nurse acknowledges the difficulty that Mr Waters is having in discussing the fact that he can no longer look after his wife at home. This opens up the subject so that Mr Waters can begin to articulate both his feeling of tiredness and the misery of the situation that he is in.

The skilled use of silence supports the effective use of questioning in that multiple questions are avoided and due time is given for the patient to respond to questions as they arise.

Touch

The use of touch in interactions is largely dictated by cultural norms but is also influenced by individual differences. Argyle (1983) sees touch in the British as something that is little used, except with close friends and partners. He suggests that hand touching is the most that is likely to happen between those who do not know each other very well, and argues that one can tell the closeness of a relationship by the zones on the body which are open to touch. In other cultures, different norms apply; in some, hugs and kisses, which in Britain would be seen almost as a sexual embrace, are considered a normal social greeting.

Recently, there has been a growth of interest in the concept of therapeutic touch (Kreiger 1979). Exponents of the theory of the therapeutic value of touch will argue that hugging a patient who is distressed will comfort and reassure him. In this respect touch can be seen to be linked with empathy. What must be accepted is that it is not easy to use touch in a therapeutic way if the individual is unused to being touched by anyone who is not very well known to him.

Some individuals touch very few people. They may, as Argyle suggests, shake hands but do no more than that. At the other end of the continuum are those who greet everybody with a kiss. If, in Figure 5.1, (1) represents the end of the continuum, where touch is not very much used, and (10) represents the point where the individual kisses everybody as a greeting, then every individual will fall somewhere between those parameters.

1 ——————————————— 10
Uses little touch   Touches a lot

Fig. 5.1 A touch continuum.

The two people involved in any interaction can be by nature at any point on the touch continuum. This means that if a health professional attempts to develop a 'touching' approach in an interaction he or she may well be rebuffed by individuals who are low on the touch continuum. Similarly, if a health professional appears to be very cold and distant, he or she may be misinterpreted by a patient who is up towards 10 on the touch continuum. Given these wide variations in feelings about touch the maxim should perhaps be, 'if it feels right do it'. Touch should be spontaneous if it is to be empathetic and therapeutic and it must feel comfortable for both parties concerned.

It is vital that any professional who does use touch a lot is very aware of the responses that this invokes from the patients or relatives concerned. This should avoid any misinterpretation of the meaning of touch.

Mr Carter was very distressed after the death of his wife. Nurse Edwards hugged him spontaneously, both at the time of death and at his wife's funeral. After two bereavement visits, Mr Carter invited Nurse Edwards to call him by his Christian name, and on a subsequent visit, invited her to dinner. Nurse Edwards found herself in difficulties because her warmth had been misinterpreted and as a result, transference had occurred, i.e. Mr Carter was putting Nurse Edwards into his dead wife's place emotionally and sexually.

Finally, it is important to remember that a therapeutic interview does not have to include touch. Health professionals who in their normal lives touch only a few very close people should not feel guilty because they are uncomfortable with using touch as a part of their professional behaviour.

Gestures

Most people use gestures to amplify or illustrate the words that they are using. In this respect hands, head, or the whole body can be used to express what an individual is feeling as he talks. Again, there are wide cultural differences that come into play, but gestures are important because they can give considerable information about how somebody is feeling.

In interpreting an individual's response to touch, for example, it will be his gestures that give clues to the way he is responding. For example, if a health professional attempts to hug a patient and that patient withdraws his body, moves his head to one side, and puts his hands up as if to ward the health worker off, then he is giving a clear indication that he does not wish to be touched. Similarly, when an individual is explaining certain situations, the gestures that accompany his words can give insight into, for example, the depth of his worry.

Health professionals need the skills to be able to interpret the gestures which their patients make. A quiet patient who has turned his face to the wall, for example, may be labelled as 'withdrawn', his non-verbal message amplifying other clues that he does not wish to interact with others at present.

Hands are particularly expressive. Individuals can show openness by holding their hands with the palms outwards; they can ask others to keep their distance by putting their hands up as if to say stop; or they can give the impression of self-protection and/or aggression by folding their arms, or by clutching each arm with the opposite hand.

The difficulty with gestures, as with all other non-verbal behaviour, is in their proper interpretation. Here it is important to link non-verbal with verbal behaviour. Just as touch can be interpreted as anything from a friendly gesture to a sexual advance, according to the verbal messages that accompany it, so gestures can mean anything from a simple expression of feeling to something much more complex.

The individual who sits with arms tightly folded and with hands clasped on opposite arms may simply be cold. However, if the gesture is accompanied by angry words and an unhappy expression it may well be a clear message that the individual is closing off from the interaction for one reason or another. If there is ambiguity in the messages then the health professional should acknowledge the ambiguity and seek some clarification of what is happening.

In any interaction, each individual responds to the gestures of the other. Just as the health professional can interpret and explore the patient's gestures, the patient will be trying to make sense of the gestures made by the nurse or doctor. This gives health professionals a responsibility in terms of what will come across from them to their patients. Health workers should therefore attempt to become aware of their own gestures. Closed gestures will give the patient the impression that the health professional is not attending to him and this in itself can diminish the chance of the patient disclosing his worries and concerns.

The skills of interpreting non-verbal responses may be improved by careful observation and by responding to one's own gut feelings about the interaction. If, for example, a patient's body language suggests that they are finding it difficult to express feelings, the health worker might acknowledge this. The patient's confirmation will build confidence for the future while denial and/or elaboration will aid learning and insight.

Eye contact

A lot can be assumed from whether or not individuals look at each other when they are talking. There is a common belief that someone who will not look another person in the eye is shifty or has something to hide whereas the individual who makes good eye contact is honest. Without considering the truth of this belief we may simply note that good eye contact in an interview will help the patient to feel that his problems are of interest, and he will therefore be much more likely to disclose what is on his mind.

In developing good eye contact with patients it is important to distinguish between what *is* good eye contact and what constitutes staring at a person. If a gaze is held for too long then the other individual will begin to feel very uncomfortable and in some way cornered. This links with the argument that if a health worker is going to maintain good eye contact with a patient he or she cannot do that and take notes as well. In fact, if notes are taken as headings (see p. 24) this activity can be used to strike a good balance between maintaining eye contact and giving the patient relief from the health professional's gaze.

Eye contact, as any other part of an interaction, is not one-sided. It is important to develop the skill of reading the patient's eye contact behaviour. If, for example, a patient is maintaining reasonably good eye contact and then suddenly looks away and seems unable to meet the health professional's gaze, it may be that there is an important reason for this which needs exploring.

Nurse:	I wonder if you can tell me just what's worrying you, Mr Waters?
Mr Waters:	Well, it's all this talk of yours about me being tired.
Nurse:	Can you tell me some more about that?
Mr Waters:	(looking away, mumbling) I can manage.
Nurse:	I just get the feeling, Mr Waters, that you're very uncomfortable with this conversation.
Mr Waters:	(defensively) What makes you think that?
Nurse:	Well it's as if you can't look at me anymore.

In this exchange the nurse acknowledges Mr Waters' difficulty in being faced with his tiredness, which is inevitably going to lead to his wife needing respite care. Generally, patients do not object to such acknowledgement, for it gives them time and space to explore their feelings. Mr Waters, for example, will be able to tell the nurse that he is thoroughly miserable and rundown but feeling very guilty. This will allow a subsequent exploration of the possibilities for Mr Waters and his wife.

Lack of eye contact can be due to shyness, discomfort, and even hostility. Some clues to the cause of eye contact behaviour can usually be gained by the accompanying verbal messages. If not, and there is a mismatch of messages, then the reason for the mismatch must be explored.

When discussing very personal issues it is worth remembering that in normal society individuals are not encouraged to disclose personal matters. The individual may therefore not be accustomed to articulating his feelings and for this reason alone it might be easier if he is not actually looking at the health professional. This needs to be accepted, for commenting at that point on a lack of eye contact might well impede the patient's story. However, when the disclosure is complete it sometimes helps to acknowledge how difficult it has been for the individual:

Mr Waters:	Well, I'm glad I've got that off my chest, Nurse.
Nurse:	Good, and I just guess that you found it very, very difficult.
Mr Waters:	Yes, afraid that's why I couldn't look you in the eye.
Nurse:	Please don't worry about that.

Here Mr Waters, having articulated his way through a very difficult problem, is able to acknowledge just how difficult it has been. The nurse's comments about the difficulty are interpreted as a very empathetic response.

Posture

Posture, as many other aspects of non-verbal behaviour, can be almost wholly unconscious. It is interesting to note that children very often adopt postural behaviour similar to that of their parents. In interaction, posture is important because it will affect who is in control of the interaction and how the individuals concerned relate to one another.

When a patient is lying in bed the posture of the nurse or doctor who talks to him is very important and needs active thought if the patient is to feel comfortable in the interaction. If a doctor or a nurse comes to the bedside and stands talking to the patient lying in bed, the patient either has to look up to see the face that is hovering above him, or retain his normal level of gaze, which will be fixed at a point somewhere midline of the nurse or doctor. A nurse talking to Mrs Mayes, asked her what she had understood from the doctor when he discussed her operation. Mrs Mayes chuckled and said, 'I hope you don't think I'm rude, Nurse, but he just stood there towering over me and I felt a little bit uncomfortable; and then I found that my eyes were just fixed on the zip on his trousers. I must admit that, you know, it all washed over me after that.' The nurse was

amused and later told a colleague that she would think more carefully in future about how she stood in front of patients.

Sitting on the edge of the bed, if a patient cannot get up, can give quite a degree of reassurance, since it demonstrates interest and concern and makes for a more comfortable interview. There can be good eye contact, and if appropriate there can then be touch; these elements can restore the balance in the interaction. If, on the other hand, the patient is up and about, then in any interaction it should be ensured that both individuals are sitting at an equal level. This requires that some thought be given to the chairs that are used. If, for example, the patient sits beside the bed and there is no other chair, the health professional may sit on the bed. This will mean, however, that the health professional is sitting at a higher level than the patient, which may be interpreted as the more powerful position.

Many interactions are so short that in fact there is no time, nor would it be appropriate, to gain equal seating, equal eye level or the comfort of both parties. What should always be possible is a warm and facilitative posture. For example, a nurse may come into the ward and ask a patient if he feels ready for a bed-bath. The nurse may unthinkingly stand hands on hip, and this may be interpreted by the patient as an aggressive, demanding stance that gives him no room to decline the offer of a bath. Developing a facilitating posture is a matter of projecting how a particular stance will be interpreted by the patient; where possible, it should also entail ensuring equality in terms of eye contact so that the patient does not feel overpowered.

Posture must be interpreted in conjunction with the verbal messages that accompany it; this is as true for the patient as it is for the health professional. But if a patient is cowering in bed while maintaining that he is not worried about anything, it is probably the cowering that is the stronger and more accurate message. The health professional needs to check on the mixed message, for example by saying, 'Well Mr Smith, you say you are not too worried, but you look very worried. I wonder if you can tell me some more about that?' Alternatively, the message may be mixed in the opposite direction, such that the patient explains fears and worries while maintaining a very relaxed posture. Again, this needs to be acknowledged. For example, the nurse might say, 'Well Mr Smith, you say how worried you are, but you look very relaxed. I wonder if you can tell me which of these messages I should believe?'

Interpretation of non-verbal behaviour

It can be seen that in all areas of non-verbal behaviour interpretation is of great importance; perhaps here, more than with verbal messages, is there room for serious misunderstanding. Where verbal and non-verbal behaviours seem to be in conflict our natural tendency is to believe the stronger message — which is normally the non-verbal one. If communication with patients is to be effective the interpretation of conflicting messages should not be left to chance. Most patients are only too willing to explain what they really mean, or how they really feel, providing that they feel themselves in an environment that encourages trust and honesty. It is very hard not to make assumptions, but by making *any* assumption we may miss an important message, and the chance to understand how the patient is feeling.

It is also essential that the patient is not confused by the messages coming from the health professional. The nurse who asks the patient if he 'wants' a bath must really *mean* that he has a choice. Similarly, in an assessment interview, if the nurse says 'Tell me how it feels' she must then be prepared to wait and hear just how it *does*

feel for the patient. If her non-verbal signals suggest that she is not interested in the patient, then she will educate him to respond at a superficial level. Concentrating on non-verbal behaviour and its meaning is something that is not commonly given time in social interaction. It can, however, give an individual considerable insight into the behaviour, priorities, and real beliefs of others.

Summary

In this chapter the significance of non-verbal behaviour has been considered, along with the links between it and verbal interaction. It has been suggested that there are non-verbal skills which can be developed. These include listening, the active use of silence, the use of touch, and an awareness of the significance of gestures, eye contact and posture. It has not been suggested that these skills can be taught, but rather that they can be developed with insight on the part of each health professional.

REFERENCES

Argyle M 1983 The psychology of interpersonal behaviour, 4th edn. Penguin, Harmondsworth
Argyle M 1988 Bodily communication, 2nd edn. Methuen, London
Davis B, Ternulf-Nyhlin K 1982 Social skills training. Nursing Times Oct 20
Faulkner A 1984 Teaching non-specialist nurses assessment skills in the aftercare of mastectomy patients. Unpublished Ph D thesis, University of Manchester (Steinberg Collection, Royal College of Nursing)
Krieger D 1979 The therapeutic touch: how to use your hands to help or heal. Prentice-Hall, Englewood Cliffs, New Jersey

EXERCISES

1. Take a large piece of paper and draw a straight line on it marked equally from nought at one end to 10 at the other. Go round your colleagues on the ward and ask each of them to place themselves somewhere on the continuum in terms of their comfort with touching other people who are not very close friends. Then choose a colleague that you trust and discuss with that person how you both feel about touching patients, and about touch in general.

2. Take a patient whom you plan to assess and make a conscious effort in terms of your non-verbal behaviour in the interaction. After the interview, ask yourself the following:

   a. How did you arrange the seating?

   b. How active was your listening, and how much of an effort was it to listen actively to what the patient was saying to you?

   c. Was keeping good eye contact difficult? If so, what made it difficult? If not, what helped you to maintain good eye contact?

3. Next time you are in a public place, e.g. a bus, the Tube or a restaurant, observe the non-verbal behaviour of those around you:

   a. What did you notice about eye contact?

   b. Were there matched messages in terms of verbal and non-verbal behaviour?

   c. In what ways do you think the environment was affecting the interaction?

6

Structure and focus

The skills of interviewing and the importance of non-verbal behaviour in health worker–patient interaction have already been considered. If patients' problems are to be identified in a skilled way during an interview, the encounter must be given structure and focus. In addition, there must be a willingness on the part of the health professional to explore the patient's feelings at sometimes quite a deep level; moreover, sufficient care must be taken to examine these feelings without doing the patient any harm.

Negotiation

There is an old adage that if you don't know where you are going you might end up in the wrong place. This is worth bearing in mind when managing an interview, for if someone is simply allowed to talk in an unfocused way, an incoherent jumble of facts and feelings may arise. Such a statement may well appear to conflict with the notion of a patient-led agenda, but in fact this is not so. By negotiating the structure and focus of an interview before it starts, and indeed as it progresses, the interviewer makes the patient aware of the areas that need to be covered. The patient can then exercise choice as to which areas to cover at any one time.

In real terms, the patient-led agenda that results from negotiation means that the patient suggests the bare bones of the interview while the health professional takes the responsibility for maintaining structure and focus. If at the beginning of the interview the task has been set out, then obviously that too is very important within the structure of the interview.

Cue priority

It will be remembered from page 32 that an interview based on a patient-led agenda depends very much on cues that are given by the patient. It is in picking up these cues that the professional gives focus to the interview.

In real life, patients do not offer cues one at a time, in order of their importance to them. They often give a number of cues all together and it is then important for these to be picked up and accorded their true priority. The following examples show two ways of picking up cues:

(1)

Nurse:	Mr West, you're looking very worried today.
Mr West:	Aye, I'm worried.
Nurse:	Do you want to tell me what's on your mind?
Mr West:	Oh, it's all sorts of things — this diabetes, injections every day, testing my urine and worrying about the future.
Nurse:	Don't you worry about the future, Mr West, that's why you're here. We're going to sort it all out for you and when you go home, you'll be like a new man.

(2)

Nurse:	Mr West, you're looking rather worried today.
Mr West:	Aye, I'm worried.
Nurse:	Do you want to tell me something about that?
Mr West:	Well, the injections every day, testing my urine, wondering about the future. I wonder where it's all going to end.
Nurse:	It sounds as if you've got a lot of problems there, Mr West. Which one would you like to talk about first?
Mr West:	Well, really it's remembering

	everything — head like a sieve, that's me — wonder if I'm going to be the death of myself now I've got this to cope with.
Nurse:	And is that your main worry?
Mr West:	Well yes, if I could think of some way that I'll get it organized then maybe the rest would follow. I don't know — it's a horrible time.

In the first incident, the nurse rushes in to reassure the patient that he will be all right; she gives his cue for reassurance top priority. In fact, of course, this will not reassure at all, because she has not examined properly what the patient's problems really are. In the second exchange, the nurse asks the patient to identify his most important concern and offers to explore it with him. In this way she begins to address some of Mr West's problems in a structured and focused way.

The priority that the patient assigns to the concerns he has mentioned may not match what the health professional expects. Often something quite small seems to be more important to the patient than something much larger. This is a problem for the health professional more than for the patient, who normally has a very clear idea of what worries him most.

It is sometimes a temptation for the interviewer to focus on cues that have to do with physical problems, primarily because these may be easier to deal with than social or psychological problems. The following example demonstrates this:

Doctor:	Well Mrs Mayes, all ready for your operation then?
Mrs Mayes:	Well, Doctor, I'm not too sure. It's a big thing having your breast off and I wonder how I will get on with my prosthesis.
Doctor:	You'll get on fine. The specialist nurse is going to come and measure you up and you'll manage well. You'll have a soft one to start with until you're healed and then we'll get you a

prosthesis that you're totally comfortable with. I'm sure you won't have any worries at all.

Mrs Mayes: It still seems a big thing.

Doctor: Now you worry about getting better. You leave the bits and pieces to us. I can assure you it will be alright.

In this exchange Mrs Mayes twice alludes to the enormity of the operation. Her other reference to the physical aspects of post-mastectomy rehabilitation is an easier cue for the doctor to pick up because he can reassure her that she will be well fitted with a prosthesis. This sort of behaviour does not necessarily mean that the doctor doesn't care, but it probably *does* mean that he feels safer with problems for which he can offer some concrete help than with those that require the focus to be on the patient and her fears.

Diversions

Diversions are normally offered by the patient and can affect both the structure and the focus of the interview. Diversions can have two purposes:

- to comfort the patient
- to comfort the health professional.

Comfort of the patient

An experienced interviewer who allows the patient to talk about his problems may be the first person who has given him that opportunity to disclose. This means that often the patient is articulating for the first time the things that are on his mind in the current situation. There may be some pain inherent in that disclosure which causes the patient to try to divert attention from the matter in hand. If the interviewer goes along with this digression the patient is 'let off the hook', i.e. he can avoid talking about the things that bother him. There is, however, a fine line between encouraging people to disclose their concerns and violating their right *not* to discuss issues if they really are too painful.

Comfort of the health professional

When a patient offers a diversion, the health professional is very often tempted to go along with it. The problem then is, that in going for the diversion, the matter in hand about the patient's concern, whatever it might have been, can get lost completely and not be returned to.

Health professionals need to recognize when diversions are offered. An effective interview with a patient may be very painful, for in exploring painful areas, the health professional becomes much closer to the patient's reality. This carries costs which are addressed in Chapter 10.

Diversions are one form of let-out for both patient and professional. There are several ways to handle them which both consider the sensitivity of the patient and the costs to the professional.

(1)

Doctor: Mrs Mayes, Nurse tells me that you're a little worried about your breast cancer because of your mother and the fact that she died from it.

Mrs Mayes: Yes, yes I'm worried about that. I'm worried too about my own daughter.

Doctor: Tell me about your daughter.

Mrs Mayes: Well, she's sixteen and wants to be a ballet dancer — you know what they're like at that age — and I'm just so worried for her.

(2)

Doctor: Mrs Mayes, Nurse has been telling me that you're rather worried about this operation because your mother died of breast cancer.

Mrs Mayes: Yes I am, and I'm worried too that my daughter might have it.

Doctor: Let me come back to the risk for your daughter. I want, at the moment if it's OK, to talk about *your* worries.

(3)

Doctor: Mrs Mayes, I hear that you're a

bit worried about your operation because of your family history.

Mrs Mayes: Yes I am. I just wonder what my outlook will be.

Doctor: Tell me about your mother.

In the first example, the patient offers a diversion which the doctor takes up, losing sight of the patient's problem. Here, both the patient and the professional are using the diversion and losing the structure and focus of the interview. In the second example, the doctor does not use the diversion but he does acknowledge that it is there. The patient has introduced another worry which the doctor puts on hold while going back to the task at hand, which is to confront Mrs Mayes' worries about her own health. In the third example the doctor picks up one of the cues given by Mrs Mayes and uses it as a diversion, so that he asks about the patient's mother rather than the patient's fears for herself. It can be seen that the second example is most effective in keeping the interview on course.

Maintaining focus

Maintaining focus requires the ability to negotiate, to control the conversation in a sensitive manner and to acknowledge difficulties if they seem to exist. It also requires the ability to remember those items that have to be put on hold. If the interviewer is taking notes, this last is a simple matter because problems may simply be written as headlines, starred and then raised later.

It is important that if the interviewer offers to come back to a diversion, a different cue, or another focus, he or she remembers to do so. Mrs Mayes, for example, in mentioning her concern for her daughter's future can be seen to be digressing from her own worries. That should not, however, trivialize the very real concern she has for her child. This means that the subject must be returned to when Mrs Mayes' worries about her own future have been addressed.

Occasionally a patient makes it crystal clear that he himself has difficulty in maintaining focus, particularly in a painful area. This may be obvious from the patient's non-verbal behaviour or from the patient's verbal admission that he does not want to talk about something. If, on checking, it appears that the patient really cannot talk about a particular issue because it is too painful, then that issue must be left for that particular time. However, the health professional should now be alerted to the fact that there is a worry here that may need further exploration at a time when the patient is more ready to talk about it.

Here we may return to George, who was finding it quite difficult to talk about the death of his wife (p. 31). He said that he had 'put the lid on' but the nurse, by gently exploring his feelings, did encourage him to talk:

Nurse: George, you say it's like losing a part of yourself. Can you tell me some more about that?

George: I try not to think about it, it's just so painful.

Nurse: I guess it must be but I wonder, is there anything else you do want to say?

George: Just that I wish I was dead too.

Nurse: Is that really how you feel?

George: Oh aye, I've thought about it. It's two months now — two months of not remembering that I only need to make one cup of tea. Two months of sheer hell. I want to be with her.

Nurse: Have you seriously made any plans for that?

George: Well, I've thought about it. I've thought about all that pain-killing stuff I've still got from when she was so ill. I never took it back you know. It's all there waiting — waiting for me to be brave enough and then I'll be with her.

In the above exchange, George manages to get past his pain to disclose his need to be with his wife. The nurse obviously has to refer this on, but by negotiating with George she is able to obtain a coherent picture of exactly how he feels about the loss of his wife.

EXPLORING FEELINGS

Levels of interaction

During the course of an interview which has maintained structure and focus it is very likely that the patient will begin to describe not only the facts about his current situation but the accompanying feelings too. In this respect it is useful to think of levels of interaction. The following distinguishes four levels of exchange, according to the degree to which they allow feelings to be explored (see also Table 6.1).

Level 0

Level 0 is only mentioned here to underline that an interaction can take place with absolutely no thought of feelings at all. This is very common at a social level. It is possible to meet a friend in town to say, 'Hi, how are you?' and get the response, 'Fine, how are you?'; at that superficial level the interaction begins and ends. Each person goes away having discovered nothing about the other.

This level of exchange is not uncommon between health professionals and patients, relatives or, indeed, colleagues. The nurse brightly going round in the morning taking temperatures, giving out breakfasts and making beds often operates at level 0:

> Nurse: How are you, Mr Smith? Had a good night? I bet you're looking forward to your breakfast.
> Mr Smith: Oh I'm OK, Nurse, how are you?
> Nurse: Fine.

This superficiality can also extend to interactions about quite important things such as Mrs Mayes' operation, Mr West's diabetes, or Mr Roger's coronary attack. Such exchanges only serve to educate the patient not to talk about feelings but to keep things at a light social level.

Level I (Hint of feeling)

Operating at level 1 means that the patient may give a hint of how he is feeling about a particular problem or situation. If the health professional is wishing to stay in level 1, then he or she will not help the patient to develop his discussion of the way he feels and may indeed block the subject or move on to some other area, as in the following example:

> Nurse: Hello, Mr Smith. How are you today? I bet you're looking forward to your breakfast.
> Mr Smith: Not really, Nurse, no I'm not really looking forward to my breakfast today.
> Nurse: Why is that?
> Mr Smith: Well, it's this rotten operation.
> Nurse: Oh Mr Smith, I've told you before, we'll look after you. Now come on, it's bacon and egg this morning. I'm sure you're going to enjoy that.

In this exchange, Mr Smith hints that he is concerned about the operation. He does not make that hint explicit but in fact the nurse blocks the exchange by prematurely offering reassurance. Whether or not she does this consciously, it has the effect of educating the patient that he is not to discuss his worries and concerns. It can be argued that the nurse actually does ask Mr Smith how he is feeling, but she is in fact only operating at a similar social level to the person in the street who says, 'How are you feeling?', expecting the response, 'Fine'.

In social exchanges there is little encouragement for people to disclose feelings. If an individual were to respond to the social greeting of 'How are you feeling?' with 'I'm feeling awful. I've had a terrible night. I'm having real problems and I don't know what to do about them', it is reasonable to suppose that whoever asked the question would find some excuse to scuttle off. This underpins the notion that in interviewing patients and relatives, the health professional requires skills that are quite different from social skills. It is these special skills that encourage the disclosure of feelings that is not permitted in a usual social setting.

Level 2 (Feelings mentioned)

When a patient is troubled by undisclosed

feelings he may first of all give just a hint of them, as in the previous example. To take things further the nurse, doctor or health worker needs to give 'permission' for the hint to be made explicit. Mr Smith, for example, if not blocked by the nurse when he mentions his concern, might go on to disclose the precise nature of his worry. This would require, of course, that the nurse asks him to expand on his remarks.

> Nurse: You sound worried about your operation. Can you tell me what's worrying you?
> Mr Smith: Oh, I had this horrible nightmare about the operation. It was horrible — I was sweating, I was so worried. When I woke up I wanted to get dressed and go home.

Here, the hint, i.e. that Mr Smith was worried about his operation, has now been made explicit in the description of a nightmare that worried him so much that he wanted to go home and not stay for the operation. Breakfast time may not be the best opportunity to confront such worries but obviously they do need to be explored as soon as possible. That the nurse was able to encourage Mr Smith's disclosure without blocking shows that she is operating at level 2.

Level 3 (Feelings expressed)

Exploring feelings at level 3 means helping the individual to articulate his fears and worries and perhaps to face them for the first time. This can be a painful experience both for the person with the worry and for the health professional, who must accept the sometimes disturbing feelings of the patient. Mr Smith, for example, identified that he was worried about dying on the operating table (p. 33). He had at that level hinted that he had a concern and mentioned the feeling of worry that he would not wake up. If left at level 2 he might himself dismiss the feeling as irrational and illogical. In order to help Mr Smith to overcome his fears it is necessary to find out precisely the nature of his feelings, as in the following exchange:

> Doctor: Mr Smith, I understand that because you know of someone who did die on the operating table that this is a worry for you too, but I wonder, can you tell me exactly how you're feeling about having the operation?
> Mr Smith: Well I told you, Doctor, it's not the operation — I understand about that — it's just this business about going to sleep and not knowing what's going on.
> Doctor: But how does that leave you feeling?
> Mr Smith: Well like I said, it's the nightmares and I wake up sweating.
> Doctor: Can you tell me some more about that?
> Mr Smith: Well, it's difficult. I'm there, I know I'm asleep and I'm outside myself and it's weird; it's as if I won't be able to get back into my body and I'm terrified doctor, absolutely terrified.
> Doctor: Of dying?
> Mr Smith: Of, well . . . of disintegrating, of disappearing. It's . . . oh you'll think I'm silly, it's hard to put into words.
> Doctor: Try and tell me some more about these feelings.

In this exchange Mr Smith tries hard to put his feelings into words. He uses terms such as 'terrified' — a very potent word — to show the fear he has at his forthcoming operation. He may indeed be so apprehensive that he will need help before he can happily go to theatre.

Table 6.1   Levels of interaction in exploring feelings

Level	Feeling	Example
		Response to 'How are you?':
0	No feeling	'I'm fine'
1	Hint	I suppose I'm OK.
2	Mention of feeling	I'm worried about my operation
3	Feeling expressed	I'm so worried, I'm having nightmares — me outside my body — disintegrating

Expression of feelings

Many patients are very nervous of expressing their feelings even when the health professional makes it quite clear that it is all right to do so. They may feel that their worries will seem trivial to an outsider, and that professionals are too busy to listen to illogical fears and worries. It is not always easy in these circumstances to reassure an individual that his worry is unfounded and that he can put it behind him.

To stay with the example of Mr Smith, it might be said that although such cases are very unusual, patients *do* die on the operating table. What the health professional can do, perhaps, is to put this worry into some sort of context that the individual can accept and understand. This is very different from premature reassurance, which simply dismisses the worry by saying, 'Don't worry, everything will be all right.' With Mr Smith, for example, one might say: 'Well it's unfortunate that you know somebody who did die on the operating table. It's very, very unlikely that it will happen to you, but you can be sure that we'll do everything we can.'

This may not be enough, and it may help to ask a patient who is extremely worried about something what *he* thinks would help him to deal with his concern. Sometimes this is something quite simple. At other times help is needed of a very different kind from that which the average health professional can offer. Mr Smith's worry may be so intense that reassurance is quite useless.

From the foregoing it will be seen that the exploration of feelings can occur at a number of levels. As described, these have been largely under the control of the health professional, who can block the expression of feelings at any point from the first hint of those feelings to their full articulation.

It should not be forgotten that in fact the patient himself can halt the expression of feeling at any point. Examples in previous pages show that occasionally a patient may find the subject too painful or embarrassing to talk about, or too difficult to put into words. It is here that the skills of interviewing can help a person to identify his concerns and to explore his feelings as far as he is able.

Because the subject matter is sometimes very painful or personal it is not unusual for a patient to cry in the course of such an interview. If a patient does become distressed when expressing feelings, the health professional should acknowledge that distress and check whether the patient wishes to stop.

Lifting/rescuing

In helping a patient to examine his feelings the health professional should encourage a balance between the expression and exploration of feelings on the one hand, and a downward spiral towards depression on the other. If this balance is not maintained then the patient is at risk of being left with feelings that he cannot easily handle.

Once feelings are expressed to an extent that the health professional has a clear idea of the depth of the patient's worry, then the interviewer has a responsibility to lift that patient's mood. This is sometimes called 'rescuing', in that the patient is helped to lighten his mood without the seriousness of his concerns being minimized. To achieve this the health professional must be very much in control of the situation, though in a sensitive and helpful way, as in the following example:

Nurse: Joanna, you're looking pretty upset.

Joanna: Oh, that's just me having a little worry.

Nurse: Can you tell me what that worry is?

Joanna: Well, Nurse, it's so safe in here. I'm worrying about what will happen when I go home, whether the violence is going to start all over again.

Nurse: Can you bear to tell me some more about those feelings?

Joanna: Yes. It was hell before I came in here and I know it will be hell when I go back. Sometimes I'm frightened of him and I lie in bed cringing, wondering what will happen when he comes up and yet I'm not brave enough to go in another room; and sometimes I feel so desperate, so upset and angry that I want to kill him and I'm frightened that one day I will.

Nurse: How seriously have you thought about that?

Joanna: Oh, seriously enough. I've got a plan but of course I'll never carry it out.

Nurse: Could you tell me that plan?

Joanna: No, I don't want to talk about it any more.

Nurse: But you're feeling pretty upset.

Joanna: I despise myself. Sometimes I lie here and I look at the wreck I've made of my life and I wonder where it will go from here. I just feel devastated.

Nurse: I can understand that that's very very difficult for you and I know we've talked about this before. Is there anything else that's upsetting you?

In this exchange Joanna Hope, who first appeared on page 4, first hints at her worry, then mentions her feelings and then describes those feelings and their effect on her. The nurse screens to make sure that she has a clear picture and then moves the patient on. This is what is meant by 'lightening' or 'rescuing': moving away from a difficult area, having first acknowledged that it is there and that it has been taken on board.

Joanna accepts the control exerted by the nurse, who acknowledges the difficulty and then moves on. Sometimes the patient might resist that control and say something like, 'Look, I haven't told you everything yet.' If that occurs, it is worth checking whether what has not been said should have been said. If in fact it is simply part of spiralling downwards still further, then the nurse has to exert control and again 'lift' the patient.

Of course, the patient himself might lift the situation by expressing serious and deep feelings and then, without help, moving on to the next area of the interview. Such a patient is well in control, even though he may have problems that he wants to discuss.

When an individual has been talking about his fears, worries and attendant feelings it is important to check how he is feeling afterwards. Even when the patient has been moved on to less difficult areas there may still be reverberations from the material that has been discussed. This possibility needs to be acknowledged:

Nurse: Joanna, this has obviously been a very difficult interaction for you talking about all your worries at home and the difficulties you're facing there. I wonder how you're feeling now?

Joanna: Well, it's funny but in a way better.

Nurse: Better?

Joanna: Well, I haven't been able to talk about this before, you know how it is — loyalty. You can't very well tell your own mother, his mother, certainly you can't talk to the kids, and if you do there's always that feeling that other people will think that somehow you invited violence. I feel you've let me talk about it and it's been OK.

Nurse: I'm sorry there isn't anything more tangible that I can do.

Joanna: But in talking to you my thoughts have got into some sort of order. I know now that I'm going to have to sort this out for good and all.

Not every interaction has a happy ending. That is part of the cost of caring. Joanna may go home to her violent husband and with the best will in the world be unable to resist what happens there. And although patients' problems are not always so severe as Joanna's, very often a problem as it is presented does not have a neat or easy solution. The help that the health professional can give by interacting effectively is to assist the individual concerned to clarify his or her thoughts and begin to move on to possible solutions to current problems.

Summary

Structure and focus have been considered as aspects of the interview aimed at identifying problems in a skilled way. The need to negotiate, to assign some priority to the patient's cues and to control diversions such that the focus is maintained until each sequence is closed have been considered. Different levels of exploring feelings have been suggested, along with the need to lift the patient's mood after disclosure so that he is in balance when the health professional leaves him. The cost to the health professional of interacting at these deeper levels will be considered in Chapter 10.

EXERCISES

1. Before interviewing a patient of your choice, list the areas you would want to cover professionally. Interview the patient from his perspective, then:

   a. Note the areas covered by the patient. How well do they match your professional list?

   b. Note how you maintained focus. How difficult did you find it to keep the patient in sequence?

   c. At what level were feelings disclosed?

   Note:
   If possible, tape-record your interview and ask a trusted colleague to comment on (a), (b) and (c).

2. Think back to an exchange with a patient with which you were uncomfortable. Perhaps you had the feeling that there were unidentified problems. With hindsight, how differently would you have structured the exchange?

7

Handling emotion

Many patients do not have serious emotional problems. They may need help with physical problems but in all other respects their lives are in balance. Some patients, however, do have problems; we have considered, among others, Joanna with her violent husband; Mr Smith, who is frightened of dying on the operating table; and Mrs Mayes, whose mother died of a similar condition to her own. By helping such patients explore their feelings it is perhaps possible to help them come to terms with them, but in doing so a number of emotions may be elicited which normally would be suppressed or contained in some way.

It is this deeper level of interaction that is seen by some to be very risky. A strong argument can be made that many of these problems do not have immediate solutions and therefore there is little point in helping people to talk about them. Another argument is that the feelings in question are so private that they should not be brought into the open. Such arguments suggest that there is no benefit to the patient of sharing emotions and little that can be done to make things better.

It has been seen that in assessing a patient's problems the aim is to explore with the patient areas of concern by means of a negotiated interaction, always checking that it is not too painful for the patient to disclose his feelings. Perhaps what is surprising is how welcome most patients find the chance to discuss matters that are on their minds, whether these are directly or only indirectly related to their disease.

Eliciting emotional reactions

Benefits for the patient

In looking at the benefits for a patient of having permission to articulate his feelings, we must again draw a distinction between social and professional interaction. In social interaction one is encouraged to put a brave face on things if there are problems. Individuals who do this are commended for coping well. Western culture does not encourage the show of emotions, even at times when one would expect an individual to be very upset.

By encouraging an individual to explore his feelings it is possible to acknowledge that those feelings exist, and thus to make them legitimate. It is not unusual for a patient after exploring a particular problem to say, 'You know, it was difficult talking about it but I feel somehow as if a weight's off my mind.' The health professional might feel sorry that he or she cannot take the problem away and may make this regret explicit; to this it is not unusual for a patient to respond, 'You've helped a lot, just letting me talk.'

Talking in itself does not solve problems but interactions can be therapeutic. Talking can also help to put problems into perspective even though the process of exploring those problems can be very painful.

Benefits for the health professional

At first sight it can seem that there are few benefits for a health professional in taking on another individual's emotional problems. It can be both a painful and a revealing process to become aware of another's worries and concerns, often because the patient may present as calm and content, while coping with considerable difficulties. However, in terms of identifying where a patient 'is at' at a particular time, and in terms of making sense of a patient's behaviour, finding out what his problems are and how they are affecting him can be very rewarding.

If interaction remains at a superficial level, it is difficult to tell how a patient is really reacting to his current situation. By helping him to explore his feelings it is possible to gain a more accurate picture of his response to diagnosis, prognosis and the current situation.

Even if an individual does not discuss his feelings, his non-verbal behaviour very often gives an indication as to what is going on. The problem on a first assessment is in knowing how 'normal' the current behaviour is. For example, it is possible to describe somebody as being quiet and withdrawn. If the individual was normally ebullient and full of life one would identify a change, but it has to be remembered that many people do come across as quiet and withdrawn in their normal life. They simply are not outgoing people. In-depth assessment will answer some of these questions, even on a first encounter. This then will allow the health professional to put the observed reactions into some sort of context.

While it is true that many patients are in balance about both their disease and its treatment, at the other end of the continuum some patients simply cannot cope with what is going on. This is where it is important to draw a distinction between the person who is typically quiet and withdrawn and the person who is quiet and withdrawn because of his reaction to the current situation.

It is possible to argue that any patient coming into hospital is likely to be anxious and fearful of what is going to happen to him. This leads to what is called 'normalization', whereby the health professional believes that it is perfectly normal for patients to be worried, anxious or fearful about impending treatment or about disease and its prognosis. This belief implies that no action need be taken except reassurance.

In-depth assessment in which feelings are explored allows the identification of those patients at risk of not coping with their disease and its treatment, and permits the health professional to differentiate between normal levels of anxiety and depression and those that are abnormal and require treatment.

Strategies for handling emotion

Many emotional responses are encountered by health professionals, whether from patients who are coming to grips with their disease and its treatment, from relatives who are worried and do not quite understand what is going on, or, on occasion, from co-professionals. These responses will include anger, guilt, fear, denial, anxiety and sometimes depression and suicidal thoughts.

Anger

Anger is not generally hard to identify although its exact cause may be difficult to understand. We saw earlier (p. 18) that John Rogers was angry and identified that anger as disease-linked. Later exploration by the nurse revealed that the anger was also linked with his wife's plans to leave him. In dealing with anger it is important to know its cause, whether it is justified and where it is focused. The aim is then to defuse the anger and make it more manageable for the individual.

It is not unusual for anger to be one of the responses to ill-health. Most individuals look for meaning in their lives and so when something happens that is upsetting they feel there has to be a reason for it. If there is no obvious reason then anger can result at the unfairness of having something visited upon one that has not been deserved. Mr Rogers is a good example of this in that he had a healthy lifestyle and was conscientious about exercise, healthy diet and other means to health, only to find that he had a coronary attack. He also felt that he had been a good husband and father, only to find that his wife was planning to leave him.

When someone feels that life has been unfair and that somehow they have been given a raw deal for no good reason, it is very tempting to point out to him that life is *not* fair. But this does not generally have any effect on anger since in any emotional situation it is unlikely that logic will have any immediate influence.

In dealing with anger the health professional may feel at a disadvantage. One cannot take away the unfairness of life, nor yet restore conditions to what they were before. The aim must be to acknowledge the anger, to make it legitimate, and to attempt to dispel it.

Nurse: You seem pretty angry, John.

John: Well, it's all so unfair. I've led a healthy life, don't smoke, hardly drink, I'm really healthy and I've been good to Debbie. She wants for nothing. I work all God's hours for her and I'm losing her too.

Nurse: It must seem very unfair.

John: Wouldn't you be angry?

Nurse: I guess I would in your situation.

John: It's so rotten. My brother — out drinking every night — could do with losing several stone. My sister-in-law hardly ever knows when she's going to see him, and look at his life. She dotes on him and he's as healthy as you are, Nurse. Yet me, do all the right things and this is how it is.

Nurse: Sounds as if you feel really cheated.

John: I do, I do.

Nurse: Is there anything else?

John: Only that I don't know how to put it right.

Nurse: Put what right?

John: Persuade her to stay. I'm sorry, Nurse. I shouldn't be taking this out on you.

In this sequence, because the nurse has acknowledged the anger, made it legitimate and allowed the patient to ventilate it, the anger has started to dissipate. Had the nurse chided the patient or tried to rationalize what had happened to him, the anger might well have spiralled upwards. In fact, it was coming down well in a very short time.

Focus. The focus of anger is important because it may be quite inappropriate. Occasionally a health professional is faced with an angry patient or relative who is directing his anger at some aspect of care, or at a particular professional. An individual may claim, for example, that the diagnosis was not made early enough, that treatment has not been appropriate, or that there has been some form of neglect. This can happen particularly after a death: a relative may come on the ward and be quite angry with the ward sister or the doctor because of the way in which the loved person died. What is important here is to determine whether the accusations are justified or not. If the anger is unjustified but nevertheless evident, one has to ask questions about the focus of that anger.

Archie Waters had lovingly cared for his wife in her final illness at home. He had had no help but had looked after her night and day unfailingly for some months. The community nurse, when visiting to do a dressing, noticed how tired Mr Waters was. She suggested that there should be respite care for his wife to give him a chance to gather his strength to continue caring for her.

Mr Waters agreed that his wife should go into the local hospice for a few days. Sadly, his wife died within 24 hours of admission. Mr Waters subsequently appeared at the hospice, demanding to see the ward sister. He was very angry indeed and accused the sister of killing his wife: 'I looked after her at home for months and she was all right with me. As soon as she got here she died. You couldn't have looked after her properly or it wouldn't have happened.'

The ward sister could see how angry Mr Waters was but knew that the care that the hospice had given to his wife had not contributed to her unexpected death. Her task was to locate the real focus of the anger and then try to defuse it:

Sister:	Mr Waters, I can see how angry and upset you are. I wonder if we can talk about that for a while.
Mr Waters:	There's no point talking. You killed her. It had to be that way.
Sister:	I know it's hard for you to understand just what's happened but I don't really believe that all that anger belongs with me.
Mr Waters:	I cared for her. She didn't go without anything when she was with me and then as soon as she comes to you look what happens.
Sister:	How do you really feel about that?
Mr Waters:	I shouldn't have let her come. It was selfish. I could have managed without a rest.
Sister:	It sounds as if you feel a little guilty for letting her go.
Mr Waters:	I do, I do. I'm sorry, Sister, I know it wasn't you. I suppose it could have happened but I just feel so helpless. I promised her I'd care until the end and I let her down.

In this exchange it can be seen that although Mr Waters' anger is real, much of it is anger at circumstances and at himself for taking a break from looking after his wife. Once the focus of the anger is identified and Mr Waters feels free to share his thoughts about what has happened, the anger is defused. In this instance, however, there is guilt left behind.

Effective approach
Acknowledge anger
↓
Identify focus
↓
Legitimize (if appropriate)
↓
Encourage expression of anger
↓
Anger is defused

Ineffective approach
Dismiss anger
↓
Refute focus
↓
Defend actions/colleagues
↓
Anger spirals upwards

Fig. 7.1 Handling anger.

Guilt

Mr Waters is not unusual in feeling guilty about neglecting his wife. Individuals make enormous demands on themselves when it comes to meeting the needs of others that they love. Any outsider looking at the situation logically would have known that it was unreasonable to expect any person to care for his wife with no help for months on end. Mr Waters' rest was well deserved and it was certainly unfortunate that his wife died before she returned home.

That is the logical view but Mr Waters is operating within emotional, not logical, parameters. It is not unusual for the bereaved to have guilt feelings. Most individuals wish that they had done more for the person that they loved, that they had been more considerate, more caring, less irritable or impatient, and that they had generally handled their difficult situation more effectively. It is at times of crisis such as illness, particularly terminal illness, that those feelings of guilt are likely to add to the burden of the carers.

Many patients also feel guilty; the patient who smokes who now has lung cancer is tormented by the thought, 'If only I'd had more sense; I wouldn't have brought this on myself'; those involved in accidents often have feelings of guilt that they were partly the cause of what happened. Sometimes guilt is perfectly justified but sometimes it is without foundation.

In a current study of families of childhood cancer patients, one father believed that he had caused his child's cancer. He had been involved in active service in a war and knew that he had killed people. He saw his child's cancer as his punishment for his wicked actions. His guilt weighed so heavily on him that he had suicidal thoughts which continued for some years after the child had been diagnosed and treated.

It is not normally possible to take guilt away, but by allowing an individual to talk about his feelings it is possible to put his guilt into some sort of perspective so that he may have some chance of forgiving himself for his inappropriate actions in the past.

If guilt feelings are not identified and explored they may fester, as in the case of the father of the child with cancer. Individuals burdened by such feelings may then need help from a psychiatrist before they can come to terms with their reality. The health professional's role in dealing with guilt is to acknowledge the emotional difficulty the person is experiencing and to accept the reality of the guilt. What an outsider cannot do is take the guilt away with reassurance or absolution.

Mr Waters:	I'll never forgive myself, Sister. I'll never forgive myself for letting her come here.
Sister:	I'm sorry that you feel so guilty but I wonder if you're not being just a little hard on yourself.
Mr Waters:	I don't know. I don't know how other people would have been. I was tired. I was really, really tired. That's why I let her come. I'm just not sure any more.
Sister:	Have you thought of how your wife might see it?
Mr Waters:	Oh she was special, endlessly forgiving. I guess she might have understood.
Sister:	Does that help?
Mr Waters:	Well, I don't know. It's funny you know, even getting it out of my system, putting a label to it, I feel a bit better, but I do wish she'd been with me at the end.

In this sequence the sister is not doing anything to take away the guilt but she is asking Mr Waters to look at it with new eyes and to ask himself if he is perhaps being a bit tough on himself. These strategies often help to put guilt into perspective unless it is at such a level that it needs specialist help to resolve.

Denial

Denial occurs when a situation is so difficult for an individual that he simply has to put it out of his mind as if it does not exist. In health care, denial is seen particularly with respect to disease or treatment where the future is uncertain or the outlook very poor. The individual appears to 'put the lid on' the information and then behave as if it were not true.

Denial is not uncommon in patients with cancer or with some other terminal or life-threatening disease. It can happen in relatives who do not want to accept the reality of what is happening to a loved one. In patients, denial can be seen as a coping mechanism but there is often pressure for them to face reality because of the difficulties that ensue when family members cannot be open with each other.

The difficulty that stems from a state of denial is that it becomes impossible to talk about the current situation. This may affect treatment of the disease and will certainly affect the individual's interpersonal relationships.

If denial is a coping mechanism then taking it away can be quite dangerous because it may be that the individual has no other method of dealing with his situation. The strategy here is to find out if in fact the denial is complete or whether it is ambivalent, as is often the case; that is, at one level the person may accept reality but at another level he may not. This means that one day he is very realistic about his situation and another day behaves as if it does not exist.

In looking for a 'window' on denial, it is possible to assess whether the denial is complete or whether there is some hope that the individual can move towards accepting some sort of reality. This involves asking the individual whether there is in fact any time when things look different:

Doctor: How are you feeling about things now, Jane? I know that we had a talk the other day and you seemed very cheerful.

Jane: Well there's no reason why I shouldn't be cheerful, is there Doctor? You're looking after me really well and I know that I'll be soon getting out of here good as new.

Doctor: Jane, I hope that things do go well for you but is there ever any time, even for just a few minutes, when it seems a bit different?

Jane: No, why should it? My husband's booking up a holiday for next year. We're going in the spring. I've always wanted to go to the Seychelles. I'm told the flowers are wonderful.

Doctor: Well, let's hope you're well enough to go.

In this sequence Jane is quite convinced that she is going to get better, even though in fact her prognosis is very poor. When looking for a window the doctor asks if she ever feels things will not be so good, and she is able to assure him straight away that she never has such thoughts. If denial is so complete it is best left alone. The following exchange, however, illustrates a somewhat different situation:

Doctor: Well, Jane, how are you feeling today?

Jane: Fine, fine. Come and look at this holiday brochure. My husband's going to take me away next year.

Doctor: Jane, is there ever any time when you're not quite so sure that you'll be well enough for that?

Jane: Well, sometimes Doctor I wake up early in the morning about 3 o'clock and then I do have quite a worry.

Doctor: What do you worry about?

Jane: Well I try to make sense of what's going on and it's a bit difficult because you know, I had all that treatment before but now I'm not on anything. You come and see me but you're not doing anything for me and I think of the fact that I'm not getting stronger and how sometimes when my husband comes to see me he's upset and pretends he isn't when I pick it up.

Doctor: And what does all that mean?

Jane: Well I wonder if one day I'm going to have to face the fact that I'm not getting better.

In this exchange Jane admits to times when reality encroaches; in the main, however, she is holding on to the belief that she will get well. This probably means that as time goes on her denial will be replaced by a sense of reality.

The situation is more difficult when denial is present in a relative. If a patient is going to die he can, and often does, die in denial, still clutching the holiday brochure. A relative, however, is going to live to face reality and so needs to come out of a state of denial before the event. Similarly, parents whose child has a chronic or disabling disease need to accept reality in order to be able to give the best care they can to their child. This will be considered further on page 74.

While one must accept that some patients need denial in order to cope, what the health professional needs to remember is that although one can *accommodate* denial one should not *feed* it. A patient may say, 'I'm going on this holiday next year' when it is very probable that he will not be alive to do so. The health professional should avoid deception by making a fairly neutral response, such as, 'Well I hope you'll be well enough to do that' or, 'I hope that things turn out as well as you're hoping.' This more honest approach, which will not break the denial, will nevertheless mean that if denial is replaced by reality the patient will not feel that he has in some way been strung along, and so trust between health professional and patient will be maintained.

Fear

To fear the unknown is only human. When an individual is ill, needing care, needing treatment, and faces an uncertain future, it is quite natural for him to be frightened. What is important to identify when interviewing patients and caring for them is whether their fear is within normal limits. Mr Smith, with his fear of dying on the operating table (p. 33), has fear outside normal limits. It gives him nightmares, causes him to want to cancel his operation and go home, and in fact inhibits his normal coping style.

By exploring an individual's feelings at a deeper level, it is possible to assess his level of fear about the current situation. Often in talking about what frightens him a patient will feel that he has put the fear into context. Often the reality of being in hospital and being under care will take away the fear because the reality fails to match up to the fearful beliefs that were brought into hospital with the patient.

In assessing a patient's level of fear, it is also important to determine its focus. In Mr Smith's case this is the fear of being unconscious on the operating table. With many patients the fear is of the operation itself; for others fear is focused on the effect of the illness or its treatment on relationships or other social aspects of life.

Many patients fear that their families will stop caring for them if they are no longer 'whole' and perfect; for example, patients who have mutilating surgery may feel that they are less acceptable to their partners than they were before. It is not possible to reassure them on this point because only their partners can do that.

What *can* be done is to allow patients to ventilate their feelings and to look for ways of exploring the matter with the partner concerned. The reality is that some relationships cannot withstand the strain of illness, of mutilating surgery, or of changes in loved ones, but by encouraging a patient to discuss these things with his partner, and by offering help where possible, fears can usually be contained.

If fear is found to be at a level where it is having a negative effect on an individual, it may be necessary to refer on for more expert help.

Risk factors

In helping a patient to identify his problems and to explore his feelings and emotions in reaction to those problems, it is possible to identify those patients at risk of psychiatric morbidity. Patients whose fear is totally inhibiting, patients who are anxious at an inhibiting level, and patients who are depressed or who have suicidal thoughts are all at risk and need to have their symptoms identified and to be referred on for treatment if necessary.

Summary

In this chapter, handling emotion, which results from interacting at level 3, has been considered from both the patient's and the health professional's point of view. Strategies for dealing with some of the emotions that are met, including anger, guilt, denial and fear, have been suggested.

EXERCISES

1. Next time you experience anger from a patient, relative or colleague, try to follow the steps outlined on page 64.

   a. What was the focus of the anger?

   b. Was it legitimate?

   c. How readily was the anger expressed?

   d. Did the anger dissipate?

   e. How were *you* left feeling?

2. Make a plan for an interview with a patient or relative who appears to be frightened. List the strategies you will use to:

   a. Identify the problem

   b. Identify the focus of the fear

   c. Acknowledge the reality for the individual.

8

Giving information

In previous chapters the emphasis has been on eliciting information from the patient to establish worries and concerns and levels of distress about the illness. This assessment stage is often criticized because it does not give anything to the patient. That is not strictly true, since the one thing it does give is the opportunity to articulate worries and concerns.

Many patients' concerns are linked to a lack of knowledge of their diagnosis, prognosis, and future outlook. Patients may also lack essential information about the body and how it works and how they themselves could take steps to improve their physical state. Some patients are obviously curious and ask for information. Other information may be deemed essential by the health professional but needs to be *offered* to the patient.

Information given to the patient can be divided, then, into two types:

1. information that the patient requests
2. information that the health professional feels that the patient must have.

Information that the patient must have includes educational material but it may also include news that the patient does not particularly want to hear. Breaking bad news is a particularly difficult area of giving information for the health professional, because most people prefer to carry good rather than bad news. In fact the ancient Greeks are said to have killed the bearers of bad tidings.

GIVING INFORMATION

There is little point in giving information until an assessment has been made of the patient's knowledge and belief about his illness and of his ability to absorb new information. By helping a patient explore his feelings it is often possible to get a picture of how likely he is to accept new information which may necessitate a change in lifestyle.

Information should be given at a rate at which the patient can absorb it, in a language he understands and in a form that is meaningful within his own social context. If information is not conveyed in this way the patient is very likely to misunderstand what is being said, often with very different consequences from those which were expected.

Psychologists have found that most people can only take in an average of seven pieces of information at any one time. Imagine, then, the task of educating a newly diagnosed diabetic in terms of testing urine and perhaps blood samples, taking insulin and adhering to a diet. It will take some time for the patient to adequately understand the situation that he is in and the effect of the diagnosis on his lifestyle. Yet the following kind of exchange is not unusual in hospital wards and outpatient departments.

Dietitian:	Mr West, I've come to talk to you about your diet.
Mr West:	Oh aye, well they're not giving me much in here.
Dietitian:	Well, we've got you on a proper diabetic diet.
Mr West:	Well what does that mean?
Dietitian:	No added sugar, not too much starch, half a pint of milk a day, and control over the size of portions that you eat. We'll give you a pair of scales so that until you get used to things you can weigh everything.
Mr West:	I'll look well weighing everything on the factory floor.
Dietitian:	By the time that we've had our little chat I'm sure that you'll be able to manage and take food to

work that will be all right for you.

The exchange continues with much more detail about the foods that Mr West can and cannot eat. The dietitian ends by saying, 'But there is some good news. You can eat strawberries and cream without too much worry and if you want a drink then dry sherry or champagne are the best for you. They do the least harm.' At visiting time Mr West recounts his visit from the dietitian to his wife:

Mr West:	The dietitian came round today.
Mrs West:	What did she say, love?
Mr West:	Oh, telling me what I could eat and what I couldn't eat.
Mrs West:	Well have we got to make a lot of changes then?
Mr West:	No, I don't think so. I've got to drink half a pint of milk a day. I don't think I'm going to do that.
Mrs West:	On its own?
Mr West:	Yes, she said I was allowed half a pint of milk a day. With all the tea and coffee I have I can't see me fitting it in but that's what she said.
Mrs West:	What else did she say?
Mr West:	She said I could have strawberries and cream and champagne. She doesn't know how we live, does she Doris?
Mrs West:	Doesn't sound like it. Have you ever had champagne?
Mr West:	No. Perhaps I should try some. What do you think?

Although this exchange ends with a fair amount of hilarity, it is quite obvious that Mr West has not understood that the half a pint of milk he is allowed a day is to be divided among teas, coffees, cereals, and whatever else he wishes. He has also picked up on those items of food he has been offered that do not fit into his lifestyle in any way. The end result is that when Mr West goes home he is very likely to be out of control. Luckily, someone overhears the Wests' conversation and more help is given about his diet, including a booklet giving the values of different foods.

The starting point for giving information is to find out what the patient knows or believes about the problem at hand. The dietitian for Mr West, for example, could start by asking Mr West about his normal diet prior to diagnosis. From that she could suggest modifications so that Mr West would be working from a point where he has good knowledge, i.e. of what he normally eats, to the point where he needs to learn, i.e. what is safe and good for him to eat. In this way there would be little chance of suggesting foods to which Mr West was not accustomed, nor yet of suggesting drinks that he has never even tried.

When educating a patient in this way, whether about diet, weight loss, exercise or any other facet of health, it is essential to check back with him to see if his understanding of the situation is realistic. If the dietitian were to say to Mr West, 'Can you give me some idea of how you are going to use your new diet?', the patient might confide that he does not know when he is going to drink half a pint of milk. This would allow the dietitian to clarify the situation by saying, 'I didn't mean that you were to drink half a pint of milk each day on its own. I meant that you were to use no more than half a pint in all the drinks and cereals that you have.' In this way there would be joint understanding.

It is often hard to accept that giving information to a patient, even if he fully understands the content of the message, does not mean that he will comply with what is being asked of him. Mr West may become totally aware of the constraints on his lifestyle as a person with diabetes. He will adapt to that in his own way and may decide that he does not want to stay with a diet that will keep him slim and well-balanced. He may indeed alter his insulin regimen to allow him to eat more. If information is used intelligently in this way, so that the end result is a patient who is in balance, then little harm is done. One could argue in such circumstances that Mr West is making an informed choice to modify the information he has been given.

Some patients may not comply with information that has been given them because they are not motivated to do so. Education fails in a large percentage of patients when the information concerns a major change in lifestyle. Smoking is a good example of this. A patient may understand perfectly that his smoking behaviour is affecting his health. He may accept at a logical level that a high proportion of smokers are at risk of getting cancer of the lung. He may accept at a logical level that, yes, he ought to give up smoking. His final decision, however, may well be to continue smoking.

Again, the patient is making an informed choice. He has all the pertinent information and has been warned of the dangers of smoking, but has made a conscious decision in the light of the evidence to continue to smoke in the same way that he did before. He may rationalize that family members smoked until they were 90 and died of something else. He may argue that he does not inhale very much; he may even cite instances where friends or colleagues who never smoked in their lives died of cancer. In this situation the patient, having made his choice, is now rationalizing that choice.

It is often difficult for health professionals to accept decisions made by patients in the light of evidence that has been given to them. The reality is that providing the information has been given, a check has been made, and the information has been understood, the final decision has to be with the patient.

On the whole, patients do try to conform to what is expected of them by health professionals. This is often easier if they are actually in hospital under the care of doctors and nurses and other health workers than it is at home. Mr West, for example, has little difficulty in adhering to a diet while he is in hospital. The situation may be very different when he gets home, particularly if he cannot eat what other members of the family can.

With diabetes it is hardly ever necessary to have a very different diet from that of others. A well-balanced diabetic who understands his diet can pick from a menu in any situation and manage without being conspicuously different. However, at home Mrs West may make special dishes and this may lead to problems. In this situation support from a community nurse may well be required to carry on the education that started in hospital.

The major motivation for compliance with a new regime once the information has been received and understood is positive feedback. It is all too easy to chide the patient who has lapsed from a new regime. However, small successes can be very intoxicating and if health professionals reinforce success, then the patient is more likely to keep trying to comply with a new lifestyle. This can be one of the rewards of interacting effectively with patients: not only knowing that the message, the education, has actually reached its target, but that there are positive results arising.

Answering questions

Questions can be asked at a number of levels. The patient who is being taught how to manage his disease and treatment may ask a lot of practical questions to help in both the understanding and the carrying out of new procedures. Questions at a deeper level may be to do with actual diagnosis, the outlook and what sort of things are going to happen in the future. All questions should be answered in a sensitive way that relate to the patient's or relative's reality.

Generally, the most difficult questions are those to do with diagnosis and prognosis, especially if the diagnosis is fear-provoking and the prognosis is uncertain. It is important here to give information at a rate that the patient can cope with and to give him a chance to halt the flow of information at any time. Questions asked may be regretted and the patient may need space to backtrack on what he has asked. Consider the following examples:

(1)

Ellen: Nurse, I sometimes wonder how things are going to turn out for me.

Nurse: In what way, Ellen?

Ellen: Well, I've had these treatments, I've had the operation and I thought I was going to get better but now I'm so tired and they've

stopped my treatment so I don't really think that they're doing anything for me and I know that I'm not getting better. I just think that it's coming to an end.

Nurse: Is there anything else that makes you feel like that?

Ellen: Yes, it was my son, Matthew. He visited me in hospital the other day and he just wasn't himself. He was just so upset and when I tried to find out what it was that was making him upset, he wouldn't talk to me. He just said not to take any notice and I must concentrate on getting better but he didn't look me in the eye. I know that lad, he's got something on his mind and I think it's me.

Nurse: You seem to be adding two and two and coming to four, Ellen.

Ellen: But I'm right, aren't I?

Nurse: I'm afraid you are, Ellen.

Ellen: So how long have I got?

(2)

Dave: I'm really worried about my leg, Nurse.

Nurse: In what way worried?

Dave: Well, are they going to amputate?

Nurse: Dave, what makes you ask that?

Dave: Oh please don't take any notice of me. I'm just having one of those low days. I'll be better tomorrow. I'm sure I'll be all right then.

In the first example, Ellen has been working out that she is not going to get better. She knows she has cancer; she had hoped for recovery but the evidence is stacking up and she is making sense of it. She asks her question and the nurse confirms what she herself has worked out.

In the second example, although the question is asked, Dave makes it quite obvious that he is not ready yet for the answer. In this instance the nurse is alerted to the fact that he is beginning to think about whether his leg will be amputated but that he is not yet ready to talk. This knowledge will allow her to monitor Dave carefully and pick up future cues if he does want to discuss his future and the possibility of surgery.

Dealing with uncertainty

Some questions do not have an easy answer. Ellen, for example, asks, 'How long have I got?' The only possible answer is, 'I don't know.'

For many years there was an ongoing debate about whether or not one should tell a patient that his disease is terminal. The major argument was that if you tell a patient that he is going to die, you take away what hope he has.

Such a belief puts hope into a very limited context, i.e. hope that one will survive. In fact, hope is much more elastic than that and when somebody knows that the time he has is short he is more likely to set goals for a short-term future and then hope that he will reach those goals. It may be something simple like hoping that one will live to enjoy a Silver Wedding Anniversary or a grand-daughter's marriage or indeed the birth of a first grandchild.

Only that information which the patient is ready to accept should be given. Ellen, for example, is ready to face the truth. Dave, in looking to the prospect of an amputation, is not ready to know the truth for sure.

Along with the debate on whether or not to tell the patient that his disease was terminal was the belief that if you did tell you could give him a time limit based on experience and what is known about a particular disease. In fact this sets up an impossible situation since it is so difficult to get things right; if one tells a patient that he has three months to live he may die much sooner and his relatives feel cheated. Alternatively he may die much later and live on 'borrowed time'. This too is hard to handle because usually the relatives have put everything into the time they thought they had. So how does one answer Ellen's question?

Ellen: I guessed that that was the answer. How long have I got, Nurse?

Nurse: I'm sorry but I just don't know.

Ellen: But you must have some idea of just how long it's going to be.

Nurse: Well, you're not feeling too poorly now and it may be that you continue as well as you are for some time — maybe for some months.

Ellen: So what will happen then?

Nurse: Well, you'll begin to have signs that things aren't so good and when that happens, obviously we'll make you as comfortable as we can but you'll know then that your time is becoming very limited.

In this sequence Ellen is pushing for a definite time so that she can make her plans and tidy up unfinished business. The nurse resists giving a straight answer but is quite honest in saying that 'We simply don't know how long.' She then gives markers to the patient; that is, she gives some indication of how the patient will know that things are beginning to change.

Markers

Markers allow Ellen to deal with her problems in what are for her manageable chunks of time. She may realize that there will be a few months, possibly, before she begins to feel less well. She may decide to take a month at a time and deal with things according to how she feels. A well-known cliché is 'take each day as it comes' but many people cannot be content with living their lives a day at a time. Many people like to think a week or a month or even several months ahead. By being given markers, patients can sort out their time in their own way and manage the uncertainty a little better than if they had no idea at all of how things were going. Ellen can be further helped by acknowledgement from the nurse or the doctor of how difficult it must be for her to handle an uncertain future.

Breaking bad news

There is no easy way to break bad news but a

distinction may be made between bad news that must be passed on to the appropriate person and bad news which need not be conveyed all at once. Sudden death, an accident, or something that affects an individual in the near future is the sort of bad news that must be passed on immediately. A difficult diagnosis and prognosis or an uncertain future is the sort of bad news that can be given to the patient or his relatives at a slower rate.

Strategies for breaking bad news are shown in Table 8.1. The example given is of someone breaking the news of an accident to the individual's husband. First, a warning shot needs to be fired. This simply means making a comment or statement that will alert the individual to the reality of what is going to happen. In the example given, it is a straightforward 'I'm afraid I have some bad news for you.' The statement may also be made non-verbally. For example, if an individual opens the door and finds a policeman standing there, she is unlikely to believe that he has come with good news. The policeman in his uniform acts as a warning shot, preparing the individual for the bad news that is to come.

The next step is to actually break the bad news. There is no easy way to do this. In the example given the statement is made, 'There has been an accident involving your husband.' Then the fact that he has had a head injury and is in hospital is conveyed. The message here needs to be clear and concise, without too much detail.

It is important after breaking bad news to give the individual the chance to absorb that news. There might be a reasonable silence, depending on the magnitude of the bad news. In the

Table 8.1 Breaking bad news

Strategy	Example
1. Fire warning shot	'I'm afraid I have some bad news for you.' Response: 'Bad news?'
2. Break bad news	'There has been an accident involving your husband.' Response: 'How bad is it?' 'We can't tell yet. This must be a shock for you.'
3. Give space	
4. Pick up pieces	'I must see him.' 'Shall I take you to the hospital?'

example given there is a pause followed by the question, 'How bad is it?' This poses a problem when the bad news is not definite. In this example the patient has been taken to hospital, and in fact to theatre, and at the time that the bad news is passed to his wife it is not known how serious his injuries are. Because the wife is probably shocked by the news she may have managed to retain only: (1) the fact that there has been an accident and (2) the fact that the accident involves her husband in admission to hospital.

Reactions to bad news

Individuals react to bad news in very different ways. Some people appear to remain very calm and matter-of-fact, while others get extremely upset. The fourth part of breaking bad news, as important as any of the others, is making an attempt to pick up the pieces after the shock of the disclosure. This should include acknowledging the shock of the news and attempting to find out how the individual is feeling and reacting.

It may be, as in the example given, that there is something tangible that can be offered, such as taking the wife to see her husband in hospital. For hospital personnel the bad news may be that a patient has died unexpectedly, or that an operation that was thought to be simple has turned out to be more complex. Staff must then take some responsibility for what happens to the relative after the bad news has been broken.

Mrs Hunt had a five-year-old daughter who started school and coincidentally became very tired and listless. She took the child to the doctor, who told her that she was worrying too much, but subsequently the child became very ill and was admitted to hospital as an emergency. It was thought that she had some kidney problems that needed to be investigated and treated.

Mrs Hunt went to visit her daughter the day after admission and sister asked her if she could go and see the consultant. The consultant sat her down and said, 'Mrs Hunt, your daughter has the nephrotic syndrome — kidney disease. She is very ill indeed and we're going to start treatment, but I'm afraid her outlook is very poor.' Mrs

Hunt was then taken back to see her child and subsequently went home. She later reported finding herself in a part of the city that she had never been to before; she had no idea how she got there and no idea of what had happened in the time between her interview with the consultant and finding herself in a strange place.

What had happened to Mrs Hunt was that she was so shocked by the news that she simply did not know what she was doing. Similar incidents were reported after the football stadium disaster at Hillsborough, Sheffield, where people were seen driving the wrong way down one-way streets after a crush barrier collapsed and people were known to have died.

It is not always possible for hospital personnel to take time out to look after people after bad news has been broken. By attempting to pick up the pieces and find out how an individual is reacting it is also possible to find out what his or her plans are. In the example given in Table 18.1 it is possible to offer to take the wife to see her husband. Were this not possible then a necessary question would be, 'Is there somebody who can take you?' In a hospital situation, if a relative is faced with bad news a mandatory question should be, 'How are you going to get home?' It may be that someone could be phoned to collect the relative, for someone who may be in shock should not have to drive home alone.

Breaking bad news at the individual's pace

Patients, as we have seen, are able to set the pace at which bad news is *received*. The health professional can set the pace at which bad news is *given*, by breaking it into parts; that is, the whole of the bad news does not have to be given at one time. In practice, the professional responds to the patient's ongoing reaction to the information given, adjusting the pace accordingly. Ultimately, the rate at which bad news is given is dictated by the patient, as in the following example:

Mr Atkins: Doctor, what's wrong with me?
Doctor: Well, Mr Atkins, we do have the results of your tests and I'm afraid the news is more serious than we thought.
Mr Atkins: What do you mean, more serious?
Doctor: Well I'm afraid some of your cells are not normal.
Mr Atkins: What do you mean, not normal?
Doctor: I'm afraid you've got some cancerous cells.

Here the doctor fires his warning shot by saying that the news is more serious than had been expected. He then starts to give the bad news in terms of some abnormal cells. The benefit of going through stages in this way is that it allows the patient to stop at any time that he feels uncomfortable; this gives him time to absorb what is being said and to adapt to a diagnosis that has many inherent problems.

The following example shows how this staged dialogue can be halted by the patient:

Mr Atkins: Well, Doctor, have you found out what's the matter with me?
Doctor: Yes, Mr Atkins, I'm afraid that the news is more serious than we hoped.
Mr Atkins: Well I'll leave it all to you, Doctor. I know you'll do the best you can for me.
Doctor: Do you wish me to discuss the diagnosis with you?
Mr Atkins: No, Doctor. I'll leave your work to you. I'll just cooperate in whatever you ask me to do.

Here, Mr Atkins is clearly putting up barriers, effectively saying 'I do not wish to know just how bad it is.' This is his right. The alternative, to force news on him that he is not able to take, could well result in denial and indeed the search for a second opinion. The following letter was written in 1984 by a patient who had been told the blunt truth about his diagnosis of cancer (Faulkner 1984).

Dear Millie,

Just a note to give you the latest medical report. As you know, the radiation was successful in removing the tumour from my left lung. I may also have mentioned that the treatment itself was giving me quite a bit of pain and agony. Well the reason is simply that the chemotherapy is not working, some kind of resistance has set up.

Yesterday I was at the hospital for results of X-rays and bone scan and was met by three specialists who told me they had nothing else to offer me and that all they can do from now on is to keep the pain under control. They give me three months at the outside if I am lucky. Is there anything I can do myself?

After the earlier results I was full of hope but now it's spreading into my other lung and has also gone into my spine, and they've taken away the last straw to which I was clinging. What else is there I can fight this thing with?

Sorry it's not much of a letter but I thought it best to write straight away. They have put me on methadone tablets and once they take hold I'm not sure who I am. Also there's also a chance you may know of some way to help, remote though it may be. Well Millie, I'll close now.

Love, Chris

It could be argued that, in fact, all bad news should be broken in small parts. Such a practice, however, is not always realistic. If a nurse or doctor has to phone a relative to say that the patient has died suddenly, there isn't really any way to break up the facts of what has happened. But in telling a patient about his diagnosis, it is important that he is given time to absorb what is happening. Dave, who needed an amputation (p. 72), was given time before the news was told him. His questions were answered but he dictated the pace up to a point where he was needing clear information. This use of euphemisms allows adaptation in a sensitive way and may lessen the impact of the shock to a certain degree.

Collusion

Sometimes the giving of information is blocked by another individual who may feel that the information to be imparted is best kept from the person concerned. This is of course more likely to occur if the information is bad news of any sort.

It is often believed that a person who colludes to keep knowledge from another does so because he or she simply cannot face up to the truth themselves. This may be so in some cases but collusion is much more commonly an act of love. Parents, for example, are very loath to tell their children when someone in their world — a grandparent or parent, perhaps — is dying. The feeling is that the children must be protected from bad news until the last possible moment.

The difficulty with this view is that the people who are excluded do not themselves have a chance to get to grips with what is happening. Indeed they may have already guessed what is happening but realize that it is not a subject to be raised.

The strategy for dealing with collusion is not to put any emphasis on the needs of the person who is being kept in the dark. If this is attempted then the colluder will say that he knows the individual concerned and knows that the person can't take the news and that he is doing what is best for that person.

In order to break collusion it is most effective to negotiate with the person who is colluding. He will need to be assessed in terms of why he is colluding and what the cost is to him of holding a secret. The cost is often extraordinarily high because if there is something that cannot be talked about between two people, then often other conversation and interchange is inhibited for fear that the secret will come out.

Sensitive assessment will often identify the cost of collusion as being high. What will also come out is that the colluder is prepared to pay this price. The strategy here that seems to work best is to negotiate with the colluder to talk to the other person and find out what he or she knows. It is even possible to promise that the news will not be broken as such, but that if the patient knows or has worked out what is going on, then of course the professional will confirm the reality.

The benefits of attempting to break collusion are that those concerned can then talk to each other and begin to sort out the various strands of their life and relationship that will be affected by whatever the bad news is. The most usual situation is that each party had known the reality and was protecting the other.

Breaking collusion, then, often involves three interviews:

1. With the person who is colluding to negotiate access to the other person

2. With the person who does not have the information to find out
   - what he does know and
   - what he himself believes, and more importantly
3. With the two people together.

This last may seem unnecessary, for if the health professional establishes that both parties know what is going on, then surely, one might think, they will talk to each other afterwards. But the reality of collusion is that if people have been colluding, even if they subsequently find out that each knows what is going on, they are unlikely on their own to start that difficult dialogue. A third person, who is simply there to facilitate, can make sure that the dialogue happens and that those concerned can move on emotionally. In the case of children it may mean that a family meeting is required to clear the air.

What can be expected if collusion is broken is a good deal of emotion. A couple, for example, who have always been open with each other may be colluding for the first time in their partnership. When one discovers that the other has been holding back information, then there could be a good deal of anger. This needs to be ventilated and is not usually very damaging. Although the initial reaction may be strong anger at having been deceived, later that individual may well realize that it was an act of love, and may therefore calm down considerably. If a health professional is acting as a facilitator in such a family drama, he or she needs just to be there and to allow those emotions to be ventilated.

Collusion cannot and is not always broken but when it is, painful though the experience may be for all concerned, there is usually a feeling of relief when things are out into the open that makes the effort worth while.

Summary

In this chapter the giving of information has been explored, both in terms of information that must be given to patients and relatives and information that is given as a result of patients or relatives asking questions. This has included breaking bad news and handling collusion.

REFERENCE

Faulkner A 1984 The consequence of ignorance: nurse–patient communication in: Brittain J M (ed) Consensus and penalties for ignorance in the medical sciences

---

EXERCISES

1. Choose a disease in your own speciality. Decide what elements of information the patient needs to understand in order to cooperate in care.

   a. Plan how you would give the information

   b. Decide how you would assess the patient's understanding of the information

   c. Put your plan into action with a patient who has the disease

   d. Review the effect of the information on the patient. How did it leave *you* feeling?

2. Imagine that a relative is asking for information on a patient in your care. The reality is that a serious diagnosis, with an uncertain future, has been made.

   a. Outline the steps you would take to give the information

   b. How would you begin to 'pick up the pieces'?

9

Plans for care

If an assessment interview has been effective, the health professional will have gathered considerable information about the patient and any problems that he might have. By interacting at deeper levels the professional will also have gained insight into the patient's reaction to his current problems and into any related emotional issues that are arising.

It is very tempting to look at the information obtained and to make decisions on what is most important in terms of planning care. It is sometimes difficult to accept that what seems to be a major problem to the health professional may be less important to the patient. If the patient's most pressing problem is an emotional one, for example, then any neatly prepared information about physical care will not be heard by the upset patient.

Joanna Hope, for example, expressed some worries about future management following her hysterectomy. She was used to a fairly active sports routine; she was a horse-rider and often lifted heavy bales of hay. She was also worried about problems with her potentially violent husband, who was unlikely to understand that it might not be practical to make love for the immediate future. Thirdly, she had problems concerned with management of her children when she returned home if, as she suspected, she did not feel 100% fit.

Before plans for the management of a patient's problems can be considered, priorities need to be set which involve the patient in terms of (1) what the priorities are and (2) what sort of decisions the patient wants to be involved in. Only then can useful solutions be generated to problems, and decisions made with regard to the best person to be involved in care. In some cases, the patient will be able to deal with his problems; in others, he may need help from a health professional. Some problems may be so severe that the patient needs to be referred to more expert help.

Setting priorities

The patient's priorities

It was seen in Chapter 4 that when a number of problems has been identified, each problem has to be checked with the patient to ensure accuracy. Further, it was seen that even when a problem-list appears to be complete it is important to screen for any problems that have not been divulged. If the interviewer has been facilitative then major problems should have been identified. If for any reason at all the patient has not felt free to talk openly, major problems may still be undisclosed.

Sometimes, even when a patient appears to have been very open about the problems he has, the health professional gets the feeling that something is not being disclosed. If this is so, the screening question has to be very specific. It might be, for example, that a nurse would say to a patient, 'Mr Smith, I think that I've got a clear view of the problems we've just discussed but I have this feeling that there's something you aren't sharing.' Mr Smith might reply that he has said everything he wants to say, and that is his right. It may also be, however, that Mr Smith needs encouragement to divulge things that he fears might be unacceptable to the interviewer. In screening, this may well be pursued as long as it is remembered that should an area be too painful for a patient to discuss, or indeed too personal for him to want to divulge, then he is entitled to maintain his silence.

Even if problems are few, only the patient can tell which of these are the most important. It is unlikely in a busy clinical situation that anyone's problems can all be dealt with at once. But if the professional encourages the patient to set priorities and negotiates with respect to what can be achieved at any one time, her management of the patient's care will truly reflect the needs of that individual, as in the following example:

Nurse: Joanna, I can see that you have quite a few problems, some to do with your own physical health, some to do with your sexual life and some to do with your relationship with your children while you are recovering. I wonder which of these are most important to you?

Joanna: Well, you won't be surprised . . . I guess what worries me most is the resumption of sexual activities. I suppose I'm a coward, I don't want to be hurt.

Nurse: I understand that but are you saying that that is the most important problem? If we can only deal with one at the moment, that's the one you want to talk about?

Joanna: Yes, though if we had got time I'd also like to start thinking about how I look after myself so that I get better as soon as possible.

Nurse: And is there any aspect of that — you getting better — that is particularly important?

Joanna: Well yes. If you read the books there's this magic six weeks and suddenly it's going to be all right, but I guess I'm worrying about what's going to happen in those six weeks in terms of, well, even feeding the horses and whether I can start to ride again, and those sorts of things.

In this sequence Joanna's problems, which had been identified before, are concerned primarily with her relationship with her husband, and secondarily with physical recovery. Had Joanna not been effectively assessed and allowed to explore her emotions the emphasis would probably have been on her physical recovery and she could have gone out of hospital still very frightened about her marriage without anyone knowing that this was her major concern.

The professional's priorities

Sometimes professionals have their own priorities for managing patient care and these may be different from the patient's. What is essential to identify in such a situation is whether the priority of the professional is so crucial that it has to be put forward to the patient, not as more important than the patient's prime concern but as equally important and for very cogent reasons.

Returning to Joanna, it may be that when she identified her major problem, that is, the fact that she would probably be expected to resume sexual activity before she felt ready, this may have been so overwhelming that she simply was not concerned about the issue of recovering her physical health. In this situation the health professional would have to negotiate with Joanna to explain the importance of physical health as well as emotional problems:

Joanna: My main worry is having to make love again before I feel ready. It's painful down there and, like I've said, I don't think I'll persuade him.

Nurse: I can understand that that's a major problem for you. Of your other problems is there anything else particularly that you would like to consider and discuss?

Joanna: No, it blocks out everything else. I'll struggle along as long as I can think of some way of managing.

Nurse: Well, we'll talk about that but one other thing I think we must talk about before you go home is how you're going to manage your physical health. You've given me a number of problems and I think we'll have to deal with some of those. Is that all right?

Joanna: (small laugh) Well, I guess if I'm feeling a bit better I might not be quite so upset over this other thing.

In this sequence the problem that the patient sees as of greatest import is that of her marital relationship, so much so that her other problems, although identified in the assessment interview, have been laid to one side. The professional is able to persuade her that some of those other problems are equally important to Joanna's convalescence and recovery. Most patients will accept that sometimes there are areas where the professional can see an importance that the patient cannot.

Sometimes the professional will identify priorities which the patient has failed to recognize as problems. In this situation the health professional will have to give the patient good reasons why he needs information about various aspects of his disease and its management that he perhaps had not thought of himself. Sometimes this activity is called 'patient education' but more generally it is a matter of alerting patients to potential problems within their situation and giving them some help in dealing with them.

Involving patients in decisions

There is a growing belief that patients should be 'partners in care'. In such a model, the patient, having expressed problems that he has, will then work with the health professional to make decisions on appropriate care. This is an ideal situation which is neither understood nor accepted by all patients.

Inevitably, most patients see the nurse, doctor or other health professional as an expert in his or her particular field. When a patient first goes along to a general practitioner because he does not feel well or because he has some anxiety about a bodily function, he goes asking for expert advice in the same way that he would go to a joiner if he wanted a floor repaired in his home or new kitchen units fitted. When offered alternatives as a result of investigation the average patient may well be very nervous of not making the right decision, as in the following example:

Consultant:	Mrs Mayes, we've investigated your lump and I'm sorry to tell you that it is malignant but we do have choices about what we should do. We could, to be absolutely safe, remove your whole breast, but there's growing evidence to suggest that if we just removed the lump, at this stage in the disease the outcome will probably be as good as if you had a mastectomy. I wonder what you would rather do?
Mrs Mayes:	Well, I don't know Doctor. Surely that's a decision for you.
Consultant:	Well, no. This is a decision that you can make. You may want to preserve your breast because if we just take the lump out then you won't need a prosthesis or anything else. There'll be a little pitting there but nothing very much.
Mrs Mayes:	But Doctor, what if it went wrong? I'd never forgive myself.
Consultant:	Well, this is your decision.
Mrs Mayes:	I'm sorry Doctor, I want you to make that decision. I'm worried enough as it is. I don't want to be involved in this.

In this sequence the patient, feeling considerable concern about her future with breast cancer, is not able or willing to make the decision about her operation. Many patients feel quite differently. They want to be involved and if that is the case then what is important is that they make an *informed* choice. The consultant who talks to Mrs Mayes in this example is not really giving her enough information on which to base a decision. In her case, of course, no amount of information would change her mind, given that her mother died of cancer. She simply wants somebody else to make the decision rather than to carry the responsibility herself. In other cases, where there is enough information for the patient to make an informed choice, the individual may well be prepared to become involved in decision-making.

Problems for professionals

A patient's involvement in decision-making can cause problems for the professional if his decision is not that which the health professional thinks is best for him. Dave, for example (p. 72), has broken his leg in a motorbike accident. There have been considerable problems in healing because of splintered bones and the decision has to be made as to whether the leg should be amputated. The consultant is of the firm opinion that this is the only possible solution. However, to get Dave to understand this and to agree to it means some negotiation and explanation of the true facts of the matter before allowing Dave to make an informed choice.

Dave is very nervous of amputation, not only in terms of the operation itself, but of the effect on his long-term future, including his ability to gain a meaningful partnership with someone who will understand that he is no longer 'whole'. Negotiating with Dave over the situation is likely to help him to make what is the best decision for him. The alternative — to tell him that the leg *has* to come off — could well set up problems in that Dave might feel so strongly that he starts asking for other opinions:

Dave:	Well, Doctor, what's happening over this leg? It's been going on a long time now and I'm a bit worried.
Consultant:	Well, Dave, I wanted to talk to you about this. I'm afraid that we've got to amputate.
Dave:	Got to amputate? What do you mean 'got to'?
Consultant:	I'm sorry old boy, it's the only answer.
Dave:	We'll see about that.

In this sequence Dave is being faced with a decision that he has not been involved in and cannot happily accept. In this sort of situation, Dave could well discharge himself from the hospital and go to other sources — perhaps paying privately — when a sensitive encounter such as the following would have been much more productive:

Dave: Well, Doctor, it's gone on a long time now. What are we going to do about my leg?

Consultant: Well, you know that we've tried very hard to get your leg to set so that it would be useful to you in the future. It's beginning to look increasingly as if we're not going to succeed.

Dave: What's that mean?

Consultant: It means that if we continue you will always have a badly deformed leg with risks of problems in the future.

Dave: So?

Consultant: Well, probably the most effective solution would be to amputate but I'm not sure how you'd feel about that.

Dave: Not good, but are you saying that it's the only way out?

Consultant: Well, what I *am* saying is that it is probably the most effective way out, but obviously you have to be happy with that decision.

Dave: That's ripe isn't it, how could I ever feel happy, but I guess I have to trust you and yeah, I'm fed up of being in and out of hospital and not being able to do things. I suppose you can fit me up with a peg-leg?

Consultant: We can do some pretty good things these days but I know this isn't going to be easy for you.

In this sequence the consultant is being honest with Dave. He is not saying that amputation is the only answer but rather that it is probably the safest and most effective answer. Dave respects the consultant and so consents to the amputation.

The problem for the professional comes when the solution that the patient takes is not the one that he or she knows to be best. This can happen in situations where a patient who has had a coronary attack, for example, is overweight, a smoker and a heavy drinker. The health professional can give good reasons why the patient should change his lifestyle but, if the patient makes an informed choice to continue with his accustomed lifestyle, the health professional has to accept this. What is important in decision-making is that the person who makes the decision takes the responsibility for doing so.

This is a general principle in medicine. If a patient comes with a problem to a doctor, the doctor diagnoses that problem, suggests treatment and does so in the belief that that treatment is the best available for this individual at this time. Should anything go wrong, the doctor will have to defend the treatment that he prescribed. In much the same way, nurses take responsibility for their decisions on standard daily patient care and on dealing with problems that arise.

If, as a result of negotiation with and explanation to a patient about options for care, the patient then makes a decision that the health professional would not have made, it is essential that the patient realizes that he is taking that decision by himself in full knowledge of any potential implications. In an ideal world this would be the obvious way to look at responsibility for actions taken. In the real world, of course, things may be rather different.

Mrs Mayes, for example, may be the sort of person who would want to make her own decision. She might be in a situation where the consultant tells her that having her lump removed would probably be as safe as having a mastectomy but that the mastectomy was the best possible option. Mrs Mayes may then make her own decision to have the lump removed and say to the doctor, 'I'll take the risk. I think it's OK.'

Subsequently, Mrs Mayes may get metastases and then it would be very easy for her to blame the doctor for not insisting that she have her breast removed. If this is a potential situation it must be very well explained to the patient what risks he or she is taking. The most appropriate decisions are normally made when there is good negotiation and understanding between patient and health professional, although there are always patients who feel that the quality of their life is more important than its duration; such individuals may well make decisions that will shorten their life.

Probably the most difficult decision-making comes when a patient or indeed a relative asks for treatment that is not appropriate. This happens particularly in terminal care where relatives often believe that another course of aggressive treatment could well tip the scales and reverse the terminal nature of the disease. It is also not unusual for relatives of patients in hospices to ask that drips are put up, or that food is forced upon an almost unconscious patient.

In situations such as this, careful assessment is required to find the real motivation for the request. Very often it is that the relative is hoping for a miracle and thinking that extra treatment or care will somehow bring that miracle about. When given a chance to express their feelings and concerns, relatives will very often apologize, backtrack, and admit to themselves — perhaps for the first time — that they don't want the inevitable to happen. Consider the following:

Mrs Treece: Sister, I'm very worried about my husband; he isn't eating any more and I can't get him to drink.

Sister: Well, no, Mrs Treece, I'm afraid he's too ill now to be very interested in any sort of diet.

Mrs Treece: But he needs to eat. Can't you put up a drip, can't you get him something that he can take?

Sister: Mrs Treece, what do you think would happen if we did put up a drip?

Mrs Treece: I'd believe that . . .

Sister: You'd believe . . .?

Mrs Treece: Oh, Sister, I can't bear it . . . I just can't bear what's happening.

Sister: It's difficult for you, I do understand that, but let's talk a little bit about what we can do.

In this exchange, Mrs Treece is painfully having to face the reality that her husband is so ill that he cannot eat. By talking things through she will be able to move on to the realization that what her husband needs now is not necessarily food and drink but to be allowed to meet death in as dignified and as peaceful a manner as possible.

Generating solutions

Patient-generated solutions

When a patient presents with physical problems which result in the need for treatment and care, it is usual for the health professional to work out the best possible options for that individual. This does not mean, as we have seen, that the patient will accept these options but simply that the health professional has made his or her decisions on the basis of the information given. In this respect the patient, quite rightly, can see the health professional as the expert in the field and may or may not want to be involved in final decisions.

It has been seen, however, that many problems that patients present concern their psychological welfare or their social life. Once it has been established that either of these sets of problems has a bearing on a disease and its treatment, then it is necessary to generate solutions for them as well.

Here, however, the health professional may not know enough facts to generate solutions. This can present a problem to those who have been taught that their aim is to take a problem-solving approach to patient care. It is probably in this domain that the patient can be truly a partner in care if he feels safe enough to divulge sufficient information about the problem and to work out, with help, what would best assist him to deal with that problem. In this activity, which may have an element of counselling in it, the health professional has three aims:

1. To encourage the patient to generate his own solutions to the problems identified
2. To suggest solutions in the absence of ideas from the patient
3. To refer the problem on to someone more expert in a particular area, if necessary.

Joanna's major problem, as we have seen, is an emotional one, i.e. her relationship with her husband.

Nurse: Joanna, you say your major problem is your sexual relationship when you go home. Can you tell me a little more about that?

Joanna: Well, like I said before, he's not very thoughtful and he will expect me to resume our normal relationship when I get home and I'm frightened that I won't be ready.

Nurse: Well, clinically we suggest to patients like yourself that love-making resumes when *you* feel ready. There isn't a magic day when it's all right and it wouldn't have been all right the day before. The average time after operation before a woman feels ready to make love is usually round about six weeks, so that means you've got another few weeks when it's perfectly all right for you to feel that, yes, it wouldn't be the thing for you to do.

Joanna: Yes, but how do I explain it to him so that he'll leave me alone?

Nurse: Well, what do you think might help?

Joanna: Well, in my worse moments I think leaving him would help, but the reality is we've got kids and I think we need to stay together, but I can't think of anything because we've been through all this before.

Nurse: Have you talked to him?

Joanna: No. Perhaps I could do that; perhaps I could say to him that I need to recover. Do you think I could do that?

Nurse: Well, yes. Talking to him might help. Can you think of anything else that would help?

Joanna: I wonder if you could have a word with him ... well just to say that it will be a few weeks before I'm allowed to make love again.

Joanna is attempting to look for solutions in a difficult situation. Because her husband is violent, she has over time stopped trying to reason with him when they are in dispute; in hospital, however, thinking about the future, hoping to preserve her marriage, she generates the idea that perhaps talking to him would be the first step. The nurse then offers to have a word with him before Joanna goes home if she is still worried.

Professional solutions

A professional solution should be offered only when the patient has exhausted all ideas of what might work, or indeed, has not had any idea at all of how to proceed. Mr West (p. 52) is very concerned with the problem of organizing his life so that he remembers when to take his insulin, when to test his urine and blood, and when he can have dietary allowances and in what proportions. On assessment he appears to have no idea at all as to how he can absorb all of this new material into his lifestyle. His reality is that he is so overwhelmed by his new diagnosis that he simply cannot think ahead to how he might manage and be stable.

The solution here that is offered by the nurse is that he should draw up a timetable of an average day and then within that timetable, with help from those health professionals concerned in his care, insert times for insulin, meals, urine and blood testing. Mr West thinks this is an idea that might work and agrees to work on the timetable and to try it out for a few days.

The risk is that the nurse may be offering something that, for one reason or another, will not fit in with the way that the individual normally runs his life. This means that if a professional has offered a solution, it will have to be checked at every stage whether the solution is working or not:

Doctor: Well, Mr West, I'm glad you've agreed to work out a timetable and I'll certainly help you to put in all the important things about managing your diabetes. Do you think this will work for you?

Mr West: Well, now that you've suggested it, I can't think why I didn't think about it. It's the way I do most things that I could forget. I keep a chart up in the potting shed so that I know when I should be planting things and when I should be transferring and all that sort of stuff, and this is going to be a bit the same, isn't it? I could put it in the kitchen.

Doctor: Yes, except that this is a daily thing and I guess your beans and stuff are more spread out throughout the year, and the benefit of the way we've looked at it is that you'll soon get into a routine that suits you and then perhaps you won't need to look at your chart every day.

Mr West: Yes, but what about the unusual days, Doctor? What do I do if I've got visitors or I'm over at my daughter's, or maybe out to dinner?

Doctor: Well, let's talk about that now.

Mr West, in working out how he is going to organize his life so that he does not forget his regimen, has a solution that he realizes would suit him very well; a new problem surfaces, however, namely what to do on unusual days. This once again demonstrates the dynamic, ongoing business of assessment and planning care.

Family solutions

Sometimes solutions to a patient's problems can in fact involve the family. Mrs West, for example, needs to be involved in planning Mr West's day. If she has his chart on the wall, she can help him to remember his diet and she can also be involved in planning his meals and making sure that, although they are not completely different from everybody else's, he nevertheless stays within safe limits.

A problem arises when a family solution is in conflict with a solution which the patient or in-

deed the health professional has generated. Mrs Treece's solution (p. 84) to her husband's illness is to force food and fluid into him, whereas the professional solution is to keep his mouth moist but to stop forcing him to eat at a particular stage. By negotiation the dilemma is solved and Mrs Treece is able to face the reality that her husband is very close to death. All conflicting solutions are not resolved so readily but in any situation where the patient has a solution and the family do not agree with that solution, the answer has to be negotiation and sometimes compromise.

One area where there often is family conflict is in the care of elderly people. Many elderly people living on their own are proud and independent but there may come a day when living alone becomes dangerous to the individual and extraordinarily worrying to the family. In these situations the family often override the solutions to the problems that have been worked out by the elderly individual.

Miss Parsons was 80, single, lived alone and was very independent. As she became older, her sight began to fail so that she could not see very well. This affected her mobility and also her ability to cook and clean and look after herself. In order to manage as well as possible, Miss Parsons cleared all unnecessary furniture from the rooms that she commonly used and in order to manage to eat without mishap, brought in a lot of ready-made meals that simply needed to be put in the oven. She had her single bed brought downstairs so that she did not have to negotiate stairs and kept a covered slop pail in the corner so that she did not have to go upstairs to the bathroom.

Her nephew, when visiting her, was aware that she was not as comfortable as she should be. The house was becoming dirty and unkempt. He felt that his aunt was not getting proper nutrition and that the slop bucket in the corner tended to be smelly. John Parsons, like many children of elderly people, made the unilateral decision that his aunt should be moved into his house. The result was a disaster. John had children and a working wife; he and his wife were very proud of their home and had brought their children up to be very fussy. Miss Parsons was very unhappy and although John's decision had been made with the best possible motives, it was the wrong decision for his aunt.

Miss Parsons confided in the district nurse, who had been brought in to care for her, that she did not like being in a house where she dared not do anything for fear that she would offend. By now the damage had been done for it was not possible to arrange for Miss Parsons to return to her own home. In this situation the district nurse was faced with helping John Parsons and his aunt to make the right decisions given the situation at that time.

Assess
↓
Prioritize problems
↓
Encourage patient to generate solutions
↓
Set realistic goals based on 'best' option
(from patient's perspective)
↓
Evaluate
↓
Re-assess

Fig. 9.1   From assessment to management.

If several solutions are generated by different individuals for any one problem, the solution of the individual who has the problem should be the one that is followed, provided that it is practical to do so. Miss Parsons, for example, wanted to go back home but it was agreed that she could not manage there any more. John Parsons felt an obligation to his aunt in that she had been very good to him in his youth and although he and his aunt both wanted the same thing, i.e. that his aunt should have the best possible quality of life, they could not agree on the best solution. Considerable work was then required between the district nurse and John Parsons to reach a compromise whereby his aunt went into sheltered care without him feeling in some way that he had failed her.

Occasionally problems may seem insoluble, such as that of Joanna and her violent husband. This is usually because logical solutions (in this case that Joanna should leave her husband) do

not fit in with the emotional needs of the individual. Health professionals can offer to listen and to help where possible but they must accept that occasionally there is no easy way out of a particular situation.

The skills of referral

Occasionally a patient presents with a problem that is not so much insoluble as beyond the expertise of the health professional concerned. When this occurs the health professional has to consider who might best help with a particular problem. If, for example, the problem is that of clinical anxiety and depression, psychiatric help may be required. In the case of emotional or marital problems it may be that some type of therapist can help.

George (p. 54) had a major problem in his bereavement because he wanted to be with his dead wife. That type of problem is usually beyond the skills of health professionals in general clinical practice and may need the skills of a trained bereavement counsellor.

Referral cannot be effected without the consent of the patient. Consider the following exchange:

Nurse: I'm concerned that you're planning to take action so that you can be with your wife.

George: I wouldn't worry, Nurse. I don't think I'll ever be brave enough but I've got all those drugs and one day . . .

Nurse: I wonder if you need to talk about this some more, and I'm not at all sure that I'm the best person to help you. Would you be prepared to talk to somebody else?

George: What sort of somebody else?

Nurse: Well, we've got a psychiatrist on our team who works a lot with bereaved patients. I think he might be able to help you.

George: You mean a bloody shrink?

Here, George immediately latches on to the fact that what is being offered is psychiatric help for his depression and suicidal thoughts. The nurse has to negotiate further to help George to understand that psychiatry is not simply about helping insane people but is about helping people who have seemingly insoluble problems or who are in a psychological state where they are at risk either to themselves or to somebody else.

It is often argued that it is not necessary to spell out the status of the person to whom the patient will be referred. But to fail to be honest about this could cause problems in the future. The status of the person should be clearly explained and any misconceptions about his or her role clarified. If, as a result, the patient does not wish to see a psychiatrist, psychologist or any other therapist, then that is his absolute right as long as he is making an informed choice. There are few altruistic suicides but if George is really bent on joining his dead wife, that is his right, difficult though it might be for health professionals to accept.

It is important to remember that referral does not equate with failure on the part of the professional who is referring, whether doctor, nurse, social worker or other health professional. Each has his or her own area of skill and expertise; each is a member of a larger team; and each should be prepared to accept that sometimes he or she is not able to help the person in question without referral to another agency.

Summary

In this chapter the use to which assessment material is put has been considered, firstly in terms of setting priorities based on the patient's perception of what is most important to himself. The use of patient-generated, and agreed, problems to set priorities has been considered, along with the potential differences between what may seem to be most important for the patient and what may be seen to be important by the professional. The concept of patients as partners in care has been described, along with the problems that may arise if too much is expected of the patient, who may not wish to take responsibility for decisions on care.

Generating solutions to perceived problems has been discussed in terms of helping patients to generate their own solutions, suggesting professional solutions where others are not available, and dealing with conflict where family solutions do not match those of the patient or the health professional. Finally, the need to refer has been discussed.

EXERCISES

1. After assessing a patient's problems, discuss plans for future care from the patient's perspective.

   a. What are the patient's priorities?

   b. Was the patient able to generate any solutions?

   c. Did *you* generate any solutions?

   d. Were goals agreed and set?

   e. Did you set a date for reassessment?

2. Think of a patient with problems who was not cooperative in terms of complying with the treatment regimen agreed for him:

   a. Was his decision 'informed'?

   b. How did the situation leave *you* feeling?

10

Dynamic interaction: process and costs

When problems have been identified and solutions generated, no matter by whom, decisions have to be made on the most appropriate solution to an individual's problem. From here, goals can be set and outcomes discussed in terms of what is expected of a particular solution for a particular problem. This will be followed by re-assessment of the problem in terms of how far a solution has been reached by the patient and perhaps his family. Planning care then becomes a dynamic, ongoing process.

Setting goals

The patient's reality

If goals are to be met, they must (1) make sense to the individual concerned and (2) be locked firmly in that individual's own reality. This reality base increases the chance of cooperation from the patient or relative who is trying to find a workable solution to a problem.

Mr West, for example (p. 85), is quite used to having lists in his potting shed, and the idea of learning to manage his diabetes using the same sort of method very much appeals to him. It might have considerably less appeal to someone who simply does not run his life in that way. Similarly with Joanna: from assessment it seems likely that she is frightened of her husband. To offer her solutions that require her to suddenly turn into a very assertive person would be quite inappropriate.

From the above it will be seen that even when

problems are identified, a skilled interactive approach is required to gain enough detail and knowledge of the individual with a problem to make sure that goals are set in realistic terms.

Goal definition

It is important that goals are clearly defined so that both the health professional and the patient are clearly going in the same direction in terms of what they wish to achieve by a certain time. It is often easier to define a long-term goal or aim in the first instance. For example, Mr West has a long-term goal of being a stable diabetic with a normal, active life. In order to reach that long-term goal, shorter-term goals need to be set, but at all times the overall goal will remain the same.

Long-term goals are not always as easy to set as those for Mr West. He aims at solving a physical problem with help, without his social life being too disrupted and without psychological problems arising. When problems have emotive overtones, such as Joanna's fears for her recovery from hysterectomy, the long-term goals might be more difficult to define. For example:

Nurse: Joanna, I think we've got your major problems sorted out and now I wonder if we can work towards setting goals for your recovery?

Joanna: Well, yes I'd like to do that.

Nurse: Well OK. What would you say was your long-term goal? What do you want to achieve overall?

Joanna: I'm not sure. I suppose what I want overall is that I can preserve my marriage in a good enough state to bring up the kids without too much discomfort.

Nurse: OK, that's a long-term goal for you. Can we now look at your long-term goal in view of your recovery from your hysterectomy?

Joanna: Well in a way they're linked, aren't they, because if I can get through the next few weeks without him hurting me, and start to feel strong again, perhaps I'll be moving towards what I've wanted for a long time from my marriage.

Nurse: OK. Let's work with that.

In this sequence, Joanna's priority is still to somehow make her marriage work a bit better. The nurse has to gently steer her back to making goals for physical recovery. The long-term goal eventually agreed for Joanna's physical recovery is that she will be able to resume all aspects of her physical and social life without discomfort. Joanna's personal addendum to this is that somehow the exercise will strengthen her very shaky marriage.

From the definition of a long-term goal, short-term goals need to be set. As the patient works towards each short-term goal he will have a sense of achievement, rather than working very slowly towards a long-term goal, which could leave him feeling quite defeated.

Managing time

When setting short-term goals it is worth thinking about how long one would expect to take to reach a particular goal. Again, the idea should be to work within the patient's own time-frame so that each individual is working within manageable chunks of time for him or her. The patient should have some influence over this proposed time-frame; otherwise, the health professional may set time limits that appear to be reasonable but which somehow disregard the needs or abilities of the patient.

Mr West, for example, might start to manage his diabetes while he is still in hospital. He could, for instance, undertake his own monitoring of blood sugar levels. The nurse should then negotiate with Mr West about the short-term goals of learning to test his blood sugar levels and remembering when it should be done, and should also negotiate the interval after which some evaluation of his efforts should be made.

Nurse: Now you know how to test your blood sugar, Mr West, why don't we organize it so that you do it while you're in here over a period of time. We'll write it down on the paper just like it'll be when you're at home on all the other aspects, and you do it each time and we'll see how you go.

Mr West: Well, you mean for the rest of the time I'm in here?

Nurse: Yes, that's right.

Mr West: But would you check it?

Nurse: Well, I thought we'd have a look in say two or three days' time.

Mr West: That's no good to me Nurse, I need to know a bit before that whether I'm getting it right or not. Shan't sleep at night.

In this sequence, two or three days seems a lifetime to Mr West, who is grappling with a new skill. What he needs is to have somebody check that he is getting it right at much shorter intervals in the first instance. The outcome is that the nurse promises to do one of the blood sugar tests each day to check how it fits into the pattern of what Mr West is doing for the rest of the day. This reassures Mr West while building his confidence in his own ability to do the test.

For Joanna, the time element has to be more elastic because goals are being set for when she is on her own at home, where there will be no health professional to help her. Her next clinic appointment will be 6 weeks or so after discharge and that to her seems an enormous amount of time to be left without any support.

In negotiation, her short-term goal is to get over the first few days at home. It is possible to arrange for a community nurse to visit within a few days of Joanna's arrival at home. The eventual goal that is agreed is that Joanna will negotiate with her husband to sleep in the spare room for the first short period after arrival at home, so that she can build her strength. Because of the known violence of her husband, she is given a telephone number to ring if she feels that she is not managing to reach her goal of self-preservation.

Motivation

Both Mr West and Joanna can be seen to be highly motivated to reach their goals; Mr West to be able to eventually manage his own diabetes without forgetting his regime and Joanna to have as peaceful as possible rehabilitation after her operation. All patients are not similarly motivated. Indeed, some of the goals set for patients are set for health reasons and not particularly because the patient desires to change his lifestyle.

Perhaps the best examples of non-motivated patients are those whose habits of a lifetime are being questioned and changed. Some surgeons, for example, will not operate on patients unless they lose weight, and some consultants ask patients to stop smoking in order to aid the treatment of their disease. In both these instances the patient may purport to wish to give up smoking or indeed to lose weight, but yet not be highly motivated to do so, and here it may be that considerable education is required before short-term goals can be set.

Some patients may respond well to incentives to change their habits or to reach goals even when they themselves are not entirely convinced of the point of the exercise in spite of careful explanation by the health professionals. In such cases, the skills of assessment and negotiation are required to find out:

* what the difficulties are in setting even perhaps short-term goals
* what types of reward would help to motivate compliance.

One patient, for example, managed to drastically reduce smoking by putting 20p into an envelope every time he lit a cigarette. At the end of each week he undertook to give the contents of the envelope to the person he disliked most in the world. This strategy would not be effective for everybody but other motivators may be possible.

Reassessment

Positive feedback

Probably the best motivation for an individual to

reach long-term goals is positive feedback as he reaches each short-term goal. The results may not be perfect. What matters is that efforts are being made to reach solutions to the problems as they were presented.

Mr West, for example, after the first day of testing his own blood sugar at the times prescribed by the nurse, omits to make the test twice and has trouble on one occasion with using the blood glucose machine. It would be very easy to say, 'Now Mr West, you must remember better tomorrow because you've forgotten it twice.' This would leave Mr West feeling quite defeated. However, if the positives are stressed first, he will feel more cheerful. For example:

Mr West: I'm afraid I forgot it twice, Nurse. I was doing the crossword the first time and by the time I looked, it wasn't worth doing it. I'm really sorry.

Nurse: But let's look at your page for today, Mr West. Look, you've managed every one except those two. That's really good. If you improve tomorrow, you might remember them all, and look at the pattern — you've obviously used the machine very well and you've obviously eaten what we've given you without anything sneaking out of the locker.

Mr West: Oh I really want to get it right, Nurse. I really do.

Nurse: And of course once you are stable, you won't have to test as much as you're doing now and you can then fix the tests along with other things so that you don't keep forgetting once you've got the crossword in front of you.

Mr West: So you're not too cross?

Nurse: We're very pleased with the way you're making an effort on this.

Mr West is left feeling so positive after this exchange that he puts real effort into the next day and manages to do all the tests on time.

Joanna has a tougher time. As she had predicted, her husband feels pretty resentful that she has been in hospital and that his life has not been as smooth lately as he had wanted it, and within minutes of Joanna getting home, he verbally abuses her. Sister had a word with him and asked him to be considerate of Joanna while she healed, and he resents that too. By the time the community nurse calls a couple of days later, Joanna too is feeling that she has failed to a certain degree in adhering to the plans that she had agreed to before discharge.

Nurse: Well, Joanna, I've had a word with the hospital Sister and she tells me that you've got quite a problem on here but that you have made plans for how you're going to build your strength and manage your convalescence.

Joanna: I'm not doing too well.

Nurse: Well, tell me what has gone right.

Joanna: Well, I have managed to sleep in the spare room. Sister did well for me there. He mutters and grumbles but at the moment I'm all right.

Nurse: And the rest?

Joanna: Oh, he's just at me all the time, muttering and grumbling, but somehow sleeping on my own — I go in there, I can lock the door and that's helping a lot.

Joanna again is congratulated on being strong-minded enough to resist her husband's taunts and demands. She left a very difficult situation when she went into hospital and has to be reminded that nothing drops into place overnight, but she now feels that she is able to have space at night and her fear of being hurt physically has abated for the present. She also feels that she can somehow work at other things at a different pace.

Both Mr West and Joanna now have something positive, their first goals having been reached in part, that they can build on. They can begin to look for ways forward, setting new short-term goals to move them on towards their long-term goal.

Renegotiation

Sometimes, for one reason or another, short-term goals are not met and renegotiation has to take place in order to determine what might work rather better. There was, for example, a risk that Joanna's husband would have overridden her need to sleep alone for a while after her discharge from hospital. If this had been the case, then no amount of motivation on Joanna's part to improve matters and manage her convalescence in the best possible way would have worked. The nurse might then have had to negotiate a new short-term goal, perhaps convalescence somewhere away from her husband, possibly by taking the children for a holiday to stay with her mother for a while. This was one of the options that Joanna had discarded in favour of trying to solve her problem in her own home where she felt that eventually life was going to have to go on.

The patients discussed in this section both felt that they had the support of the carers who were looking after them, but also felt that they were left to see how their own solutions worked. This control over what they did is an important element of moving an individual on from a problem to a potential solution and its evaluation.

In the case of problems that have no obvious solutions, the role of the carer is to help the person concerned adapt to the changes in his life and to leave him in as much control as possible of how he handles his new situation, and adapts so that he can make the most of whatever opportunities he might have. This is particularly the case in terminal care, where the patient faces the reality that time is short and his relatives and loved ones are perhaps coming to grips with the fact that he will not be with them for very much longer.

In these situations health professionals can often feel that somehow they are not offering very much when they help people to identify their problems, but the one thing that professionals do give in these instances is permission to talk, along with acknowledgement of how difficult it is to face these particular problems.

The costs to the carers

Nurses, doctors and other health professionals are usually seen by the public to be dedicated people whose aim in life is to help those who have disease and who are facing fear-provoking diagnosis and perhaps uncertain prognosis. The reality is that health professionals are human beings. They hurt like other human beings and they feel like other human beings. The more effective the health professional is in communicating with patients and their relatives, the closer those professionals will get to their patients' pain. This can have quite a high emotional cost.

Accepting a patient's reality

There is a cost to accepting a patient's reality. Often the solutions that patients see to their own problems are not the solutions that the health professional using logic would advise. It can take real effort for the health professional to allow a patient to pursue a particular solution when he or she has real knowledge that there are dangers inherent in that decision.

Nurse Jackson, who was concerned with Joanna's care, had been married to a violent man. Although he was not violent in the way Joanna's husband was, there were enough parallels between the two situations that Joanna's story reactivated Nurse Jackson's memories of her own past. She had left her husband because he had eventually turned his violence on the children as well. It can be argued that Joanna's story would leave anyone upset but Nurse Jackson was particularly so; eventually, she asked Sister if she could care for another patient and hand Joanna over to someone who would be less affected.

Some health professionals find that they do become over-involved in their patients' problems and that they take the problems home and become stressed on behalf of someone that they feel they personally cannot help. This too can take its toll. At a more pragmatic level, health professionals can become upset when patients are non-compliant in treatment. Acceptance at a personal level that health care is demanding and that carers need support can help to alleviate potential problems arising from emotional distress.

Professionals who find the cost of caring too high may resort to alcohol or drug abuse. They may also experience difficulties with their own personal relationships. The Americans use the term 'burn-out' (Maslach 1981) to describe what happens when individuals have paid too high an emotional price for the job that they are trying to do.

Signs of strain

In order to work at the best possible level, health professionals need to note any signs of strain in their work so that they can stop and take stock of problems that might be arising or difficulties that need action.

Loss of enthusiasm. When a job that has previously been interesting and exciting suddenly seems to becomes a chore, in that tiredness creeps in part-way through the day, or the particular families that the health carer is involved with suddenly seem to be very difficult, a loss of enthusiasm may result. The individual may then begin to feel that he or she is doing more than anybody else and that colleagues do not understand the enormity of the problem-load that he or she is carrying (Bernard 1991).

Loss of positive attitude. This can be characterized by 'awfulizing', that is, by finding that everything about life is 'awful', whether it's the weather, what one had for breakfast, what the traffic was like on the way to work and any other aspect of the day. Anyone who begins to habitually describe day-to-day activities as 'awful' is probably overstrained. Even close relationships become negative if this is the case.

Feeling unwell. Here there are general feelings of tiredness, headaches, lack of sleep and minor ailments. The professional may start taking time off to go to the doctor for small ailments that previously would have been taken in her stride.

Decrease in efficiency. Because the professional is not feeling well, or positive, or enthusiastic about life, he or she very often becomes less efficient on the job and perhaps shows bouts of temper or becomes offended for no obvious reason. This can lead to an inability to relate positively to patients, to families or indeed to colleagues and personal friends.

Loss of confidence and self-esteem. The individual who is overstrained in his or her post, feels unwell and is not working very efficiently, eventually, because of these increasing symptoms and reactions, loses self-confidence and gets the feeling that nothing is going right any more and that no one seems to care.

Depression. If strain is allowed to continue to the level where there is loss of efficiency and an accompanying loss of confidence and self-esteem, the individual may well begin to show signs of clinical depression. If this happens, help is required, both medical and therapeutic. These symptoms are described as the signs of impending burn-out in that the individual can no longer mobilize internal resources to deal with everyday pressures.

The difficulty with strain in a post is that the signs of that strain could easily be signs of something else; indeed, anyone who is feeling unwell and unhappy should certainly consult a doctor to rule out any physical illness.

If a professional is showing signs of strain, either by losing enthusiasm, feeling unwell or relying on alcohol or drugs to get through the day, help is required sooner rather than later. Too often colleagues will protect a colleague who is suffering in this way, feeling that the difficulties encountered if such problems become public will be too great for him or her to bear. This is short-sighted, since the longer problems are left the more difficult they are to resolve. Carers should give as much attention to their own mental and physical health as they do to that of their patients. In this way, burn-out or strain can be minimized.

Survival strategies

Survival strategies can be both personal and professional but should also include some knowledge of oneself so that limits can be set that are realistic for the individual and which will prevent over-involvement in care to the extent that the health worker is at risk.

Personal strategies

Social adjustment. Everyone has his or her own particular techniques for unwinding at the end of the day. These techniques make a clear cut from working to being off duty. They may include simple things like having a bath, changing one's clothes, sitting with a drink, watching television or talking to a friend or partner. The important thing here is not the amount of energy expended on the change-over period but that it is a total break from work.

Driving from work to home in a car can well make the break very definite, as can walking home or going on the bus. Each of these activities allows space between work and home. What is important is the wind-down so that one does not arrive home with all the problems of the day still weighing on one's mind.

This period also gives some privacy providing that it is used in a sensible way. Modern communications are such that this privacy can be invaded if each individual is not careful of it; for example, cars can be invaded by cellular phones, and patients can sometimes obtain a doctor's or a nurse's home telephone number — these all invade privacy and prevent the split from work to home that is so healthy. The colleague who, when asked what she would do if given a cellular phone for a present, replied 'I'd advertise it as an unwanted gift' was not simply joking but was saying, 'My car is one of the places where I can be me and nobody can demand anything of me.'

Hobbies. Hobbies provide useful survival strategies and time should be made to fit them into even the most busy life. They include walking, music, sport and many other activities; some are energetic while others are more relaxing. Their function is to switch attention from the pressures of life to other activities.

Hobbies, no matter what they are, encourage creative abilities that are different from the skills used in day-to-day activities. This use of creativity can be immensely soothing, especially if the hobby uses physical energy.

Time out. Hobbies allow time out from the activities of work. However, sometimes work can be so demanding that a complete break is required, even if only for a short time. For example, sometimes in terminal care several deaths occur in a row or the workload becomes particularly heavy. It is important at times of strain to recognize the individual's own need to either take a few days off or to ask for a change of scene.

A young midwife, Penny, went to see her mother one day and stated that she had a particular need. She was very interested in communicating and counselling, and consequently was given all the mothers to deal with who had difficult births, stillbirths, and Down's syndrome babies. Penny said, 'What I need is a normal delivery.' Penny's problem was that she had too heavy a load in terms of mental strain. Because she was good at what she did, her load was increasing. She needed time out and on advice went to her manager and negotiated a more balanced workload. She was then well able to continue enthusiastically in her job.

Managers can argue that it is difficult to change staff around, that staff are there to meet patients' needs and that one has to take the rough with the smooth. This is a short-sighted policy because the longer one stays in a stressful situation, the less likely one is to be able to cope with it. Time out should be the right of every health professional at times of heavy workload or recurring difficult problems.

Humour. A healthy sense of humour can be a wonderful survival technique, particularly the ability to laugh at oneself. This does not include the sick humour that makes fun of tragedy but rather an ability to see the lighter side of life. Laughter can be very infectious and is not inappropriate in a work setting. Patients enjoy sharing a joke and are often charmed to hear amusing tit-bits from the health professionals' day-to-day activities outside the work setting.

Sharing. There is an old cliché: 'A problem shared is a problem halved.' Although this is not entirely true, it *is* true that being able to talk over difficulties can help to resolve them. A friend, partner or colleague who is prepared to listen can be enormously helpful in day-to-day work but this should be a two-way relationship.

The ground rules for sharing at a one-to-one level should be quite clear so that one person is not doing all the listening while somebody else unburdens himself. If this occurs, the listener then becomes overloaded and a vicious circle can be set up. Similarly, when one has a problem that needs discussion, it is easy to believe that no-one else has such a problem. The colleague that is chosen to share that problem might also have problems of his or her own and then, without proper negotiation, there can be a competition for 'who tells first'.

Nurse Gardner described how she was driving home one day, having had a very tough shift; nothing had seemed to go right and she felt she really had not managed as well as she could. She planned how, when she got home, she would share this with her partner and she knew that he would be happy to pour her a drink and listen. In fact, when she got out of the car at her home, her partner came out of the house and said, 'Thank God you're here; wait 'til you hear the hell of a day that I've had.'

The important thing in sharing is that worries are articulated rather than bottled up inside where they may ferment and subsequently seem much worse than they really are. Often in the course of conversation, solutions that were previously elusive suddenly become obvious and the individual is then encouraged to go back to deal with the problem.

Professional strategies

Time out, sharing and humour can be both personal and professional survival strategies, but professionally one of the most useful keys to survival is to feel that one is working within a supportive environment.

A professional support group can help care-givers to cope with their work and lessen the stress of caring for the terminally ill. Such groups need an experienced leader and agreed ground-rules. These will include the topics that are admissible to be covered, a fair distribution of time so that one person does not take everyone else's attention, and agreement on confidentiality (Faulkner & Maguire 1988).

Another strategy that health professionals find quite difficult is setting limits on their involvement in their work. This requires that each individual knows his or her own limits and capacity for dealing with patients' problems.

Too often, performance is rated against the person in the team who comes to work earliest, goes home latest and appears to put most into the day. In fact, each health professional is different and each has to learn what he or she can give and still survive. In this paradigm, over-involvement is as worrying as under-involvement in work.

The key to coping with demanding work lies in knowing and accepting limitations as part and parcel of each individual. This will sometimes mean saying 'no'. If, for example, an individual health professional has had difficulties within her own family, she may be unable for a while to help others. Later, however, that experience may help her to deal with similar problems. Strategies for survival may seem to advocate selfishness. A longer-term view is that if health professionals do not care for themselves, then eventually they will have nothing left to give to others.

Very occasionally, survival may mean a change of work-setting. Helen, a diabetic herself, was a diabetic specialist nurse. She finally went to see a senior colleague because she had realized that handling her own diabetes and spending every working day helping other people handle theirs was becoming too much of a strain and she was showing signs of 'burn-out'. By changing to a different community setting for six months, she then felt able to go back to the work that she really loved best. It may be, on occasion, that a change of workload needs to be a permanent one. In any event, such decisions have to be made on an individual basis.

In fact, most professionals survive very well using their own coping mechanisms and survival strategies. By being alert to potential problems, it is possible for health professionals not only to care for themselves but also to notice when colleagues are showing signs of strain and inability to cope.

Summary

In this chapter the dynamic nature of interaction, assessment and re-assessment have been examined, along with the cost to professionals of meeting patients' and relatives' needs while surviving themselves. The costs of caring have been considered, along with the signs that an individual is not coping as well as he or she has been. Finally, survival mechanisms have been briefly set out.

REFERENCES

Bernard P 1991 Beyond burn out. Nursing standard 5(43): 46–48
Faulkner A, Maguire P 1988 The need for support. Nursing 5(28)
Maslach C 1981 Burn out: the cost of caring. Prentice-Hall, Englewood Cliffs, New Jersey

---

EXERCISES

1. List your own personal coping mechanisms for dealing with difficult problems at work.

2. How do you personally make the break between leaving work and getting home so that you can relax and adapt to your social life?

3. When did you last say 'no' in a professional situation? Try to remember how you felt when you declined whatever the task was.

11

Summary

This book has taken a reality-based, contextualized approach to identifying the elements of effective communication in health care. These include planning and negotiation, managing time and optimizing the environment as precursors to proper interaction with the patient.

Planning and negotiation

Planning and negotiation have been seen as important in the assessment of patients. If an interview is imposed on an individual when he is not ready for it — he may, for example, be recovering from previous treatment or interactions — then the best possible information is not going to be obtained. Similarly, it has been seen from the health professional's point of view that if interviews are not planned and sufficient time allotted to them, then indeed it is going to be very difficult to have a clear enough space within which to actually talk to a patient so that he feels that the professional's time is his, at least for a period long enough to identify problems and then move on to their management.

Managing time

The notion has been put forward that time is not elastic in the working day. Few health professionals have a work-load that allows them to give their patients endless time, and part of the negotiation for any planned interaction has to be organized within time constraints. It has been seen, for example, that when the time-span for an interview is negotiated, priorities are much more likely to be set by the patient and less time is likely to be given to neutral or peripheral concerns.

The elements of time usage include not only negotiating with the patient, but also controlling the interview so that time is not wasted, and ensuring that all major concerns are aired.

It has also been seen that time management includes negotiation with colleagues so that interviews are not interrupted except in the case of emergency. Other elements of managing time have been seen to include screening telephone calls, putting 'Do Not Disturb' signs on the door of the interview room and pre-arranging home visits with the hope of talking to the patient alone.

Optimizing the environment

Various discussions have highlighted the need to optimize the environment for the patient, but this has been viewed very much in terms of clinical reality whether in the hospital, hospice, home or health care clinic. Privacy, for example, has been considered in terms of how to give an illusion of privacy where no actual privacy is possible. Similarly, with a view to privacy in the patient's home, strategies have been suggested to maximize the chance of talking to a patient without the distractions and interruptions created by partners, children, pets, televisions or telephones.

Developing skills

The verbal and non-verbal skills required for effective communication have been considered throughout the book. Although separate chapters have been devoted to these verbal and non-verbal skills, it has been seen that the two are interrelated and interdependent, with the proviso that should verbal and non-verbal messages clash, those most likely to be believed will be the non-verbal ones. The role of positive attitudes has underlined the discussion on skills, as has the importance of a non-judgemental approach to the variety of problems which can be identified in patients across a wide range of illnesses.

Patient-led agenda

The theory has been developed that the most realistic view of the patient's concerns and problems will be obtained by following a patient-led agenda, whereby the patient's perspective on his current situation and its outlook come from him without influence from the health professional. It has been suggested that within this concept of a patient-led agenda the health professional will focus on cues that are given by the patient and follow them through to a logical conclusion so that sequences of events or concerns being described by a patient are not interrupted by neutral material or diversions.

This approach moves away from both the medical interview and the nursing process interview whereby data is collected by following a sequence of questions which usually have a 'Yes/No' answer. By moving away from this tick-list approach, real problems can be identified and explored.

The difficulty that is apparent in following a patient-led agenda is that the patient may not cover the areas important to the health professional. Accordingly, the notion has been put forward that the professional agenda, though very important, will be picked up at the end of an interview, but only to fill in those areas not already covered by the patient. It has been suggested that if the patient tells his story in his own way, he is very likely to cover the majority of areas of importance to health professionals; if he doesn't, the health professional can either pick up the unfinished business as individual items or indeed intersperse them within the patient-led agenda, where appropriate, in response to cues which suggest particular concerns such as clinical anxiety or depression.

Identifying problems

The whole thrust of interaction in the assessment of patients' concerns has been seen as problem *identification* rather than problem *solving*, as put forward by the nursing process approach. This does not contradict the underlying philosophy of the nursing process but merely accepts the fact that some problems of importance to patients simply do not have solutions. Identifying problems is the first step towards planning care, but this does not mean that a health professional has to feel guilty if a problem does not have an immediate solution. Nor should the professional feel that it is a waste of time to identify problems unless there is a professional solution to them. Once identified, problems should be prioritized — from the patient's, rather than the professional's point of view.

The vignettes which are presented throughout the book show that what is important to the professional may not always be of greatest concern to the patient. For example, Joanna Hope with her worries and concerns about her marriage and her violent husband is seen to be far less concerned about her physical welfare.

It has been shown by the various case studies used that the problems most pressing to the patient should be those that are taken as most important by the health professional, but when the professional agenda has priorities that are essential to patient care and well-being, negotiation should take place to prioritize problems in some sort of balance.

This book does not subscribe substantially to the notion of the patient as partner in care, not because the patient's part in his care is in any way diminished, but because patients on the whole see health professionals as 'experts' who are going to help them with their problems in disease and its treatment. It is acknowledged, however, that the patient has a very important part to play in care, particularly in the area of generating solutions to some of the problems that are identified.

The patient's individuality has been a priority throughout this book. Where there are, for example, treatment options, some patients will want to choose the best option for themselves while others will want the health professional to make the decision for them. Similarly with emotional and social problems, some patients may be quite happy to generate their own solutions and deal with their own problems. These patients in fact seldom mention psychological problems to a health professional because they

are able to deal with them and therefore do not see them as current problems. When an individual does identify psychological problems, he may need to be encouraged to generate solutions but may also need some help from the health professional.

A difference has been identified between giving premature advice and helping a patient to make his own decisions given his own knowledge of his background and of other individuals concerned.

In the area of decision-making, it has been acknowledged that if a patient makes a decision that is right for him given the problem, the background and the other variables around that problem, it may sometimes be difficult for a health professional to accept this notion of informed choice. Discussion of the need to allow a patient to live with his own decisions has highlighted the need to accept him as someone who is robust; this opposes the notion of the strong professional helping the weak patient.

Management

It has been suggested that effective interaction with patients and indeed with their families can enhance the management of particular aspects of care. For example, if patients are encouraged to generate solutions to their problems, they may also be involved in deciding which of these solutions is most likely to work for them. This leads on to setting goals with realistic time-frames and realistic aims, and to the evaluation of whether the strategy chosen has indeed worked.

Within the area of management comes particular emphasis on the family. Illustrations have been given to show that the role played by the family in illness from the time the patient first becomes ill through to cure, recurrence or indeed the terminal phase of the disease is very important.

Problems occur for both the patient and the health professional when the family's ideas of what should be done for a patient are different from either the patient's or indeed the health professional's. Strategies have been suggested for negotiating with families and, where there is conflict, with patients and family members together. No promises have been made at any point in the book that patients' and families' concerns can all be dealt with in the best possible way. Some problems have no solutions. Some families have problems that have been entrenched for so long that the point of illness is not the most appropriate time for someone else to intervene and try to find solutions. What has been suggested in all chapters is that by using effective negotiating and interviewing skills, the health professional can help patients to identify and deal with more problems than was traditionally possible by concentrating on the tick-list medical or nursing process interview.

Survival

Finally, the care of professionals themselves has been considered, and acknowledgement has been made of the cost of interacting effectively with patients not only at a superficial or factual level, but at a level which encourages the patient to disclose and to express feelings at a deep level. The problems surrounding involvement in patient care have been addressed and some of the barriers to effective communication have been considered, along with the risks to health professionals of being so involved that they 'burn out'.

Each chapter has contained at least one exercise. These are designed to help readers to use the strategies suggested in the book; to test them for themselves and begin to develop their own style; to build on existing skills and to think about the problems involved in effective interaction; and to encourage the enhancement of their interactive skills.

What this book has not attempted to do is to discuss the theory of effective communication. This is well covered by a variety of texts. What one reads is a personal matter and it is much more useful to go into a bookshop or local library and browse, read a bit and then decide which theoretical approach is most appropriate to read and think about. The model underlining the content of this book is based on a number of theories. The difference between this and other texts is its reality base and the fact that it uses real case studies to illustrate the skills, knowledge and attitudes that are required for effective communication.

Resources

The following references are just a few of those available which may be useful. In addition, your librarian will help you to look up relevant journal articles, books and other material on effective interaction, both generally and in your own area of specialization.

Some useful videos are available and may be in your library. These include:

1. Assessing a dying patient

This videotape shows the skills of assessment which are illustrated by an interview with a female patient who is dying of cancer.
Part 1   Doctor/patient physical assessment.
Part 2   Nurse/patient psychological assessment.

2. Breaking collusion

The difficult area of sharing the truth when a couple wish to protect each other is addressed in this videotape.
Part 1   Doctor interviews wife of patient to elicit her concerns re husband's prognosis.
Part 2   Doctor interviews husband to assess his awareness of diagnosis/prognosis.
Part 3   Doctor interviews couple together to facilitate sharing of awareness.

3. The difficult patient

Patients are occasionally described as 'difficult' or 'withdrawn' when they may in fact be simply unhappy. This videotape shows both effective and ineffective ways to attempt to persuade a patient to share his problems.
Part 1   Ineffective interview with nurse blaming patient for being uncooperative.
Part 2   More effective interview where nurse attempts to see patient's perspective of problems.

4. The young, angry patient

This videotape shows a young woman, dying of cancer, who is trying to make sense of her current situation. Both ineffective and effective interview techniques are demonstrated.
Part 1   Doctor shows ineffective techniques of interviewing with resultant anger on part of patient.
Part 2   Effective doctor/patient interview where patient feels safe enough to air concerns and make decision about future treatment.

5. Advocacy

The nurse often finds herself in the role of patient's advocate against the doctor who may have a different perception of a problem. This videotape shows both ineffective and effective advocacy.
Part 1   Doctor/nurse battle showing how advocacy can turn into a win-lose situation for both professionals.
Part 2   Effective advocacy where nurse uses knowledge and understanding to put patient's case to doctor.

Note

Each videotape is accompanied by full teaching notes and suggestions for group discussions.

The above videotapes are concerned with cancer care but their strategies are generalizable. They are available from Professor Ann Faulkner, Trent Palliative Care Centre, Sykes House, Little Common Lane, Sheffield S11 9NE.

6. Child of a dying parent

'Pam is dying of breast cancer. Her husband, Rob, has deliberately withheld from their children, Duncan (12) and Christopher (14), the true nature of their mother's illness. This he believes is to protect them, and to protect their mother.'

Professor Faulkner negotiates access to the children and then explores with Duncan and Christopher their feelings and reactions to their mother's illness and death. It demonstrates the need to involve children in interactions when there is a family crisis.

This videotape is produced as a teaching aid for those working with dying patients and their relatives, and with the bereaved. It is produced to the highest quality and comes complete with teaching notes. It is available from Professor Faulkner, Trent Palliative Care Centre, Sykes House, Little Common Lane, Sheffield S11 9NE.

Note. The above videotapes were made possible by Help the Hospices: 1–5 were developed by Peter Maguire, Ann Faulkner and Terry O'Dowd; 6 was developed by Ann Faulkner and Serene Productions.

Further reading

Argyle M 1983 The psychology of interpersonal behaviour, 4th edn. Penguin, Harmondsworth

Bond M 1986 Stress and self awareness: a guide for nurses. Heinemann Nursing, London

Bridge W, Macleod Clark J (eds) 1981 Communication in nursing care. HM and M Publishers, London

Buckman R 1990 I don't know what to say: how to help and support someone who is dying, rev. edn. Papermac, London

Burnard P 1989 Counselling skills for health professions. Chapman & Hall, London

Davis B, Ternulf-Nhylin K 1982 The assessment of training in social skills in nursing, with particular reference to the patient profile interview. Issues in Nursing Research. Macmillan, p 121–133

Fallowfield L 1990 The quality of life: the missing measurement in health care. Souvenir Press, London

Jackson E 1989 Understanding health; an introduction to the holistic approach. SCM Press, London

Kagan C 1987 A manual of interpersonal skills for nurses. Harper & Row, London.

Knox J D E, Thomson G M 1989 Breaking bad news: medical undergraduate communication skills teaching and learning. Medical Education 23: 258–261

Krieger D 1979 The therapeutic touch. Prentice-Hall, Englewood Cliffs, New Jersey

Lugton J 1987 Communicating with dying people and their relations. Lisa Sainsbury, London

Maguire P 1988 The stress of communicating with seriously ill patients. Nursing 3(32): 25–27

Marson S 1990 Managing people. Macmillan, London

Pearson A (ed) 1987 Nursing quality measurement. Wiley & Son, Chichester

Price B 1990 Body image: nursing concepts and care. Prentice-Hall, Englewood Cliffs, New Jersey

Robinson E J, Whitfield M J 1988 Contributions of patients to general practitioners' consultations in relation to their understanding of doctors' instructions and advice. Social Science and Medicine 27(9): 895–900

Sale D 1990 Quality assurance. Macmillan, London

Tschudin V 1991 Counselling skills for nurses, 3rd edn. Baillière Tindall, London

Vachon M 1987 Occupational stress in the care of the critically ill, the dying and the bereaved. Hemisphere, London

Verby J et al 1979 Peer reviews of consultations in primary care: the use of audiovisual recordings. British Medical Journal 1: 1686–1688

Index